CiA Revision Series

ECDL®/ICDL® Syllabus 4

using
Microsoft® Office

Dawn Harvey

Bob Browell

Brian Waldram

Philip Waldram

Mark Hodgson

Published by:

CiA Training Ltd
Business & Innovation Centre
Sunderland Enterprise Park
Sunderland SR5 2TH
United Kingdom

Tel: +44 (0) 191 549 5002
Fax: +44 (0) 191 549 9005

info@ciatraining.co.uk
www.ciatraining.co.uk

ISBN-10:   1-86005-344-0

ISBN-13:   978-1-86005-344-3

Release RS05v1

First published 2005

European Computer Driving Licence, ECDL, International Computer Driving Licence, ICDL, e-Citizen and related logos are trade marks of The European Computer Driving Licence Foundation Limited ("ECDL-F") in Ireland and other countries.

CiA Training Ltd is an entity independent of ECDL-F and is not associated with ECDL-F in any manner. This courseware publication may be used to assist candidates to prepare for **ECDL/ICDL**. Neither ECDL-F nor **CiA Training Ltd** warrants that the use of this courseware publication will ensure passing of **ECDL/ICDL tests**. This courseware publication has been independently reviewed and approved by ECDL-F as complying with the following standard:

*Technical compliance with the learning objectives of **ECDL/ICDL Syllabus Version 4.0***

Confirmation of this approval can be obtained by reviewing the Courseware Section of the website www.ecdl.com

The material contained in this courseware publication has not been reviewed for technical accuracy and does not guarantee that candidates will pass **ECDL/ICDL tests**. Any and all assessment items and/or performance-based exercises contained in this courseware publication relate solely to this publication and do not constitute or imply certification by ECDL-F in respect of **ECDL/ICDL tests** or any other ECDL-F test.

For details on sitting **ECDL/ICDL tests** and other ECDL-F tests in your country, please contact your country's National ECDL/ICDL designated Licensee or visit ECDL-F's web site at www.ecdl.com.

Candidates using this courseware publication must be registered with the National Licensee, before undertaking **ECDL/ICDL tests**. Without a valid registration, **ECDL/ICDL tests** cannot be undertaken and no **ECDL/ICDL** certificate, nor any other form of recognition, can be given to a candidate. Registration should be undertaken with your country's National ECDL/ICDL designated Licensee at any Approved **ECDL/ICDL** Test Centre.

ECDL/ICDL Syllabus Version 4.0 is the official syllabus of **ECDL/ICDL** certification programme at the date of approval of this courseware publication.

CiA Training's **Revision Exercises** for **Standard ECDL/ICDL** contain a collection of revision exercises to provide support for students. They are designed to reinforce the understanding of the skills and techniques which have been developed whilst working through CiA Training's corresponding *ECDL/ICDL Standard* books.

The exercises contained within this publication are not ECDL/ICDL tests. To locate your nearest ECDL/ICDL test centre please go to the ECDL Foundation website at www.ecdl.com.

The revision exercises, grouped into sections, cover the following modules:

1   Basic Concepts of IT

2   Using the Computer and Managing Files

3   Word Processing

4   Spreadsheets

5   Database

6   Presentation

7   Information and Communication

A minimum of two revision exercises is included for each section. There are also general exercises, which cover techniques from any section within each module. Answers are provided at the end of the guide for all modules, wherever appropriate.

The Revision Exercises are suitable for:

- Any individual wishing to practise various features of the applications. The user completes the exercises as required. Knowledge of *Windows* and *Office* is assumed, gained for example from working through the corresponding *ECDL/ICDL Standard* books produced by **CiA**.

- Tutor led groups as reinforcement material. They can be used as and when necessary.

Aims and Objectives

To provide the knowledge and techniques necessary to be able to successfully tackle the features included within the seven modules. After completing the exercises the user will have experience in the following areas:

- Understanding IT theory

- Using the *Windows* operating system

- Managing files and folders

- Producing various word processed documents

- Manipulating spreadsheets and charts

- Creating and interrogating databases

- Using the Internet to find information

- Communicating using e-mail

Requirements

The exercises assume that the computer is already switched on, that a printer mouse and speakers are attached and that the necessary programs have been fully and correctly installed on your computer. However, in some applications, some features are not installed initially and a prompt to insert the *Office* CD may appear when these features are accessed.

Downloading the Data Files

The data associated with these exercises must be downloaded from our website: *www.ciatraining.co.uk/data_files*. Follow the on screen instructions to download the data files.

By default, the data files will be downloaded to **My Documents\CIA DATA FILES\ Syllabus 4 Revision Series\Module x**. The data required to complete the exercises is in the **Module x Data** folder and worked solutions for every exercise can be found in the **Module x Solutions** folder.

If you prefer, the data can be supplied on CD at an additional cost. Contact the Sales team at *info@ciatraining.co.uk*.

Notation Used Throughout This Guide

- All key presses are included within < > e.g. <**Enter**>.

- Menu selections are displayed, e.g. **File | Open**.

- The book is split into modules and then individual exercises. Each exercise consists of a sequential number of steps.

Recommendations

- Read the whole of each exercise before starting to work through it. This ensures understanding of the topic and prevents unnecessary mistakes.

- As screen shots have been captured in the UK, currencies may be shown in £ sterling. In different countries these will be shown in the appropriate currency.

- Some fonts used in this guide may not be available on all computers. If this is the case, select an alternative.

- Additional information and support for CiA products can be found at: *www.ciasupport.co.uk*, e-mail: *contact@ciasupport.co.uk*

Revision Exercises

Revision Series
© CiA Training Ltd 2005

Revision Exercises

Revision Series
© CiA Training Ltd 2005

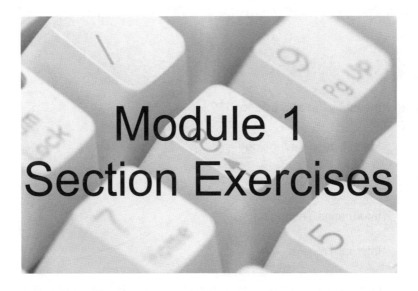

Module 1
Section Exercises

The following revision exercises are divided into sections, each targeted at specific elements of the ECDL/ICDL Syllabus 4 Module 1, Basic Concepts of IT. The individual sections are an exact match for the sections in the ECDL/ICDL Training Guide from CiA Training, making the guides an ideal reference source for anyone working through these exercises.

General Concepts

These exercises include topics taken from the following list: understanding IT, identifying computers and their uses, identifying parts of a PC and distinguishing between hardware and software.

Exercise 1.1

1. What is meant by the abbreviation IT?

    a) Identification Technology

    b) Information Technique

    c) Information Technology

    d) Internal Transfer

2. Which of the following statements about a laptop computer is untrue?

    a) It is a smaller version of a personal computer (PC)

    b) It is always powered by a battery

    c) It is portable

    d) It can be battery powered or run by mains electricity

3. A peripheral device is:

    a) Any external equipment attached to a PC

    b) A built in part of a PC

    c) A fax machine

    d) A scanner

4. In the diagram above, is the part labelled **2**:

    a)   Monitor

    b)   Keyboard

    c)   CD/DVD drive

    d)   Floppy disk drive

5. What does the term **resolution** mean?

    a)   Computer speed

    b)   A computer that provides a central storage point for data

    c)   The picture quality of a monitor

    d)   A program that allows you to use the computer

Revision Exercises

Exercise 1.2

1. Which type of computer is a large organisation most likely to need?

   a) Mainframe computer

   b) Laptop computer

   c) Personal computer

   d) Personal digital assistant

2. Which part of a computer stores programs and data?

   a) Mouse

   b) Keyboard

   c) Monitor

   d) Hard disk drive

3. What is the general term for any physical part of the computer?

   a) Hardware

   b) Software

   c) Peripherals

   d) Equipment

4. What is the general term for programs that allow you to use the computer, e.g. games, operating system, etc?

   a) Hardware

   b) Software

Revision Series
© CiA Training Ltd 2005

c)   Peripherals

d)   Equipment

5.   Which of the following devices allows you to connect to the Internet or e-mail?

a)   Scanner

b)   Keyboard

c)   Modem

d)   Central processing unit

6.   What are networked computers?

a)   Smaller versions of PCs, which are portable

b)   Large computer systems that store and process data centrally

c)   Computers held in the palm of a hand

d)   Computers connected together with cables, allowing data to be shared

7.   What does ICT mean?

a)   Instant Computer Terminology

b)   Information and Communication Technology

c)   Independent Computer Trust

d)   Information and Clerical Technology

Revision Exercises

Hardware

These revision exercises include topics taken from the following list: understanding the CPU and identifying and understanding input and output devices.

Exercise 1.3

1. Which part of a computer carries out core processing and calculations?

    a) Hard disk drive

    b) Floppy disk drive

    c) CD/DVD drive

    d) Central processing unit

2. What is the general term for a device that allows you to enter information into a computer?

    a) Input device

    b) Keyboard

    c) Output device

    d) Hard disk drive

3. Which of the following is <u>not</u> an input device?

    a) Joystick

    b) Digital camera

    c) Printer

    d) Scanner

1

4. What is an output device?

    a)   A device that allows you to see or hear what a computer is doing

    b)   A device that allows you to send information to the computer

    c)   A device that enables connection to the Internet

    d)   A device that controls the transfer of memory

5. What is a microprocessor?

    a)   A device that cooks using microwaves

    b)   A very small computer

    c)   A children's whisk

    d)   A central processing unit constructed on a single chip

6. Which of the following devices converts printed material into a digital format?

    a)   Printer

    b)   Scanner

    c)   Digital camera

    d)   Microphone

7. What would you consider to be the two most typical input devices?

    a)   Mouse and monitor

    b)   Keyboard and microphone

    c)   Mouse and keyboard

    d)   Scanner and digital camera

Exercise 1.4

1. What is the term for the speed at which a CPU can process information?

    a)   Processor speed

    b)   Clock speed

    c)   Top speed

    d)   Output speed

2. The speed at which information is processed is measured in:

    a)   Megahertz or gigahertz

    b)   ROM or RAM

    c)   Megabytes or gigabytes

    d)   Stalactites or stalagmites

3. Which device stores photographic images in digital format?

    a)   Monitor

    b)   Printer

    c)   Scanner

    d)   Digital camera

4. Which of the following is <u>not</u> an output device?

    a)   Printer

    b)   Speakers

    c)   Mouse

    d)   Monitor

Revision Series
© CiA Training Ltd 2005

5. What do you need to be able to listen to music on your computer?

    a)   Printer

    b)   Speakers

    c)   Mouse

    d)   Monitor

6. Which of the following could be classed as <u>both</u> an input and an output device?

    a)   Touch screen

    b)   Mouse

    c)   Printer

    d)   Scanner

7. What is the function of the CPU?

    a)   To connect to the Internet

    b)   To print documents

    c)   To install software

    d)   To perform all processing of information

Storage

These revision exercises include topics taken from the following list: identifying and understanding storage devices, understanding types and measurement of memory and understanding elements of computer performance.

Exercise 1.5

1.   What is the next largest unit of computer memory after 1 kilobyte?

     a)   1 Terabyte

     b)   1 Gigabyte

     c)   1 Megabyte

     d)   1 byte

2.   Which of the following statements is true?

     a)   A PC with a large hard disk drive costs much less than one with a small one

     b)   As time goes on, the hard disk capacity of new computers decreases

     c)   As time goes on, the hard disk capacity of new computers increases

     d)   Laptop computers do not need hard disk drives

3.   Which is untrue? A floppy disk can be used to:

     a)   Store 1 gigabyte of data

     b)   Copy information to a different computer

     c)   Create a backup of files

     d)   Store just over 1 megabyte of data

4.   What does RAM stand for?

     a)   Readily Available Memory

     b)   Random Assorted Memory

     c)   Random Access Memory

     d)   Random Amount of Megabytes

5. Which of the following would take up most memory?

    a)   An *Excel* spreadsheet with 100 rows of data

    b)   A single digital camera image

    c)   100 page report with graphics

    d)   100 page report without graphics

6. Which of the following will affect the performance of a PC?

    a)   Hard disk drive capacity

    b)   CPU clock speed

    c)   Amount of RAM

    d)   All of the above

7. What is the name for having several applications/processes running at once?

    a)   Multiplying

    b)   Multitasking

    c)   Crashing

    d)   Surfing

Exercise 1.6

1. Which of the following is a storage device?

    a)   Mouse

    b)   Keyboard

    c)   Monitor

    d)   Hard disk drive

2. Which storage device is portable, like a floppy disk, but can store more data?

    a)   CD

    b)   zip disk

    c)   Both a and b

    d)   a only

3. What is the process of creating tracks and sectors on disks called?

    a)   Fermenting

    b)   Forming

    c)   Tracking

    d)   Formatting

4. What is the function of read only memory (ROM)?

    a)   It stores information needed to keep the PC running

    b)   It stores information on a temporary basis, e.g. when a program is running

    c)   It is only used for reading documents or reports

    d)   It can easily be changed by the computer user

5. What is the function of random access memory (RAM)?

    a)   It stores information needed to keep the PC running

    b)   It stores information on a temporary basis, e.g. when a program is running

    c)   It is only used to access a computer remotely

    d)   It prevents the CPU catching fire

6. What is a field?

    a)   Many pieces of information relating to the same thing

    b)   A single character

    c)   8 characters

    d)   A single piece of information, e.g. a name or reference number. Several fields make up a record

7. What would take up the least storage space?

    a)   A database containing 6000 records

    b)   A spreadsheet containing 500 records

    c)   A report containing 100 names and addresses

    d)   A one page document with 30 lines of text

Software

These revision exercises include topics taken from the following list: understanding operating systems and systems development and understanding and identifying software applications.

Exercise 1.7

1. Which of the following is an operating system?

    a)   *Access*

    b)   *Windows*

    c)   *Outlook*

    d)   *Dreamweaver*

2. What does a computer do when it is turned on?

    a)   Belt up

    b)   Brush up

    c)   Boot up

    d)   Bring up

3. What is application software?

    a)   A program that ensures all other programs run efficiently

    b)   A device attached to the computer with a USB cable

    c)   Something that allows you to program the computer

    d)   A program such as *Word*, *Excel*, *PaintShop Pro*, etc.

4. Which of the following is <u>not</u> application software?

    a)   *Linux*

    b)   *Access*

    c)   *PowerPoint*

    d)   *Internet Explorer*

5. Which application would be best to use to work out your household accounts?

    a)   Word processor

    b)   Presentation

    c)   Database

    d)   Spreadsheet

Revision Series
© CiA Training Ltd 2005

6. Which application would be most suitable to produce a 10 page newsletter with text and graphics?

    a)   Desktop publishing

    b)   Web browsing

    c)   Graphic handling

    d)   Database

Exercise 1.8

1. What does a graphical user interface (GUI) do?

    a)   Displays all information in graph format

    b)   Uses icons and menus to help users perform actions

    c)   Ensures all hardware is running correctly

    d)   Performs a start up routine when the computer is switched on

2. What is an operating system?

    a)   Performs tasks on the computer and controls which processes are carried out and in which order they are carried out

    b)   A type of word processor

    c)   Specialised web browsing software

    d)   A means of performing complex mathematical calculations

3. Which type of application would you use to create the time sheet below?

	A	B	C
1	Time Sheet		
2			
3	Day	Hours	Hours to Pay
4	Monday		=B4
5	Tuesday		=B5
6	Wednesday		=B6
7	Thursday		=B7
8	Friday		=B8
9	Saturday		=B9*1.5
10	Sunday		=B10*2
11	TOTAL	=SUM(B4:B10)	=SUM(C4:C10)
12			
13	Hourly Rate		
14	Attendance Bonus		=IF(B11>20,25,0)
15			
16	Weekly Pay		=(C11*B13)+C14
17			

a) Database

b) Word processor

c) Presentation

d) Spreadsheet

4. Which type of application would you use to create the slide opposite?

a) Database

b) Word processor

c) Presentation

d) Spreadsheet

5. Which of the following processes is a major part of computer based systems development?

    a)   Testing

    b)   Browsing

    c)   Manipulating images

    d)   Chatting

6. What is the name for a fault found in a program?

    a)   Virus

    b)   Problem

    c)   Bug

    d)   Infection

Information Networks

These revision exercises include topics taken from the following list: understanding different networks and the use of e-mail and the Internet.

Exercise 1.9

1. What is the term used for two or more computers connected together?

    a)   A joining

    b)   A teamwork

    c)   A relationship

    d)   A network

2.   What is the name for a high speed Internet connection?

    a)   Headband

    b)   Broadband

    c)   Narrowband

    d)   Quickband

3.   What is a local area network (LAN)?

    a)   Only friends' computers are connected

    b)   Only computers in the same room are connected

    c)   Computers spread over a large distance are connected

    d)   Computers in close proximity, e.g. in the same building, are connected.

4.   Is the Internet:

    a)   A WAN?

    b)   A LAN?

    c)   A client/server network?

    d)   A database?

5.   Which of the following is a search engine?

    a)   Doogle

    b)   Boogle

    c)   Woggle

    d)   Google

6.   What is an extranet?

a)   A backup copy of the information on the Internet

b)   An intranet that can be accessed by authorised external users via the Internet

c)   An area on the Internet that contains sensitive information

d)   An intranet that can be accessed by everybody with an Internet connection

7.   Which of the following items can be sent as an e-mail attachment?

a)   A report

b)   A spreadsheet

c)   An image

d)   All of the above

8.   What would be the most efficient way to get an urgent sales report to your boss in head office?

a)   Send it by regular post

b)   E-mail it

c)   Print a copy and then fax it

d)   Drive to head office with a copy

Revision Exercises

Exercise 1.10

1.   What is the term used for a network in which core data is stored on a central server?

      a)   LAN

      b)   WAN

      c)   ADSL

      d)   Client/Server network

2.   Which device converts a signal from a phone line into a format that your computer can understand?

      a)   A modem

      b)   A floppy disk

      c)   A scanner

      d)   A printer

3.   If you are connected to a network, can you print files to a printer that is not attached to your computer?

      a)   Yes

      b)   No

      c)   Yes, if you can physically see the printer

      d)   Yes, but you cannot print large files.

Revision Series
© CiA Training Ltd 2005

1

4. What is the name for a special web page, linked to a database, which makes it easier to find information on the Internet?

    a)   A search network

    b)   A browsing engine

    c)   A knowledge base

    d)   A search engine

5. Which of the following is browser software?

    a)   *Access*

    b)   *Netscape Navigator*

    c)   *Outlook Express*

    d)   *Word*

6. What is an intranet?

    a)   It allows messages to be sent from one person to another

    b)   A network that can be accessed by authorised external users via the Internet

    c)   An internal network, providing web pages containing company information, standard forms, etc.

    d)   A wide area network of computers connected together

7. Which of the following is <u>not</u> required before you can send e-mail?

    a)   An Internet Service Provider

    b)   An Internet connection

    c)   Paperclips for attachments

    d)   E-mail software

IT in Everyday Life

These revision exercises include topics taken from the following list: understanding the use of computers at work and understanding the electronic world.

Exercise 1.11

1. Which of the following would be the main reason that a hospital might use computers?

    a)   To book flight tickets

    b)   To store student records

    c)   To store patient records

    d)   To buy groceries online

2. Which of the following would be the main reason that a school might use computers?

    a)   To plan timetables

    b)   To provide insurance quotes

    c)   To store details of vehicle registrations

    d)   To do online banking

3. What is distance learning?

    a)   Attending a course at a college far from your home

    b)   A course in how to plan routes efficiently

    c)   Attending a "virtual" course, i.e. over the Internet rather than face to face

    d)   Attending a course at various locations

4. What is teleworking?

   a)   Working from home using electronic communication

   b)   Working for a TV company

   c)   Working in telephone sales

   d)   Repairing television sets in your own home

5. Which of the following statements is true of e-commerce?

   a)   You can examine the goods before deciding to buy

   b)   You can pay in cash

   c)   You are able to buy goods between 8am and 5pm only

   d)   You can buy goods from almost anywhere in the world

Exercise 1.12

1. Which of the following organisations use computers?

   a)   Government departments

   b)   Banks

   c)   Hospitals

   d)   All of the above

2. What is CBT?

   a)   Computer Built Trains

   b)   Computer Based Technology

   c)   Computer Based Training

   d)   Computer Browsing Technology

3.   Which of the following tasks could a human perform better than a computer?

   a)   Perform complex calculations

   b)   Highly accurate control of machinery

   c)   Quickly manipulate data from many sources

   d)   Use judgment and common sense

4.   Which of the following tasks <u>cannot</u> be performed by a computer?

   a)   Running a police control room

   b)   Online banking

   c)   Flying an aeroplane

   d)   Choosing a personal gift for a family member

5.   Which of the following tasks would a computer perform more successfully than a human?

   a)   Retrieve a specific record from a database containing 50,000 records

   b)   Make an ethical medical decision

   c)   Give advice to a schoolchild who is being bullied

   d)   Paint a garden fence

6.   What would a government agency be <u>most</u> likely to use a computer system for?

   a)   Maintain stock control of specialist surgical equipment

   b)   Help staff to do homework assignments

   c)   Hold census information

   d)   Buy theatre tickets online

Health and Safety

These revision exercises include topics taken from the following list: identifying health and safety issues and understanding how to help protect the environment.

Exercise 1.13

1. What is the name for the relationship between workers and their environment?

    a)   Argonauts

    b)   Economics

    c)   Ergonomics

    d)   Semantics

2. Whose responsibility is health and safety at work?

    a)   The employer's

    b)   The employee's

    c)   Both a and b

    d)   The government's

3. Which of the following is <u>not</u> a common injury in an IT environment?

    a)   Injury caused by tripping over loose wires

    b)   Eye strain

    c)   Repetitive strain injury

    d)   Broken nose

4. Which of the following practices helps preserve the environment?

    a) Recycling toner cartridges

    b) Throwing away waste paper

    c) Printing every document created, rather than saving electronically

    d) Turning on colleagues' computers when they are out of the office

Exercise 1.14

1. Which of the following is <u>not</u> a health and safety requirement?

    a) Provision of adequate ventilation

    b) VDU free from flicker and interference

    c) Provision for breaks away from the computer

    d) Provision of soft drinks and snacks

2. How should a computer user's chair be positioned?

    a) So their feet don't touch the floor, but their hands are at a comfortable height in relation to the desk

    b) So their feet are on the floor and hands are at a comfortable height in relation to the desk

    c) So their feet are on the desk and their hands are comfortably on the floor

    d) So their hands and feet are on the desk

3. What is RSI?

    a)   Repetitive Stress Injury

    b)   Reading Strain Injury

    c)   Repetitive Strain Injury

    d)   Relative Stress Injury

4. What should you do first if you feel health and safety at work is not up to the required standard?

    a)   Report your employer to the police

    b)   Report your employer to your MP

    c)   Ask your employer to correct the problem as soon as possible

    d)   Look for a new job

Security

These revision exercises include topics taken from the following list: backing up, privacy issues, information security issues, understanding the implications of theft, computer viruses and anti-virus measures, copyright legislation and the data protection act.

Exercise 1.15

1. What should you do to protect your work from accidental loss?

    a)   Back it up

    b)   Pack it up

    c)   Boot it up

    d)   Brick it up

2. What can you do to prevent an unauthorised person viewing or changing your data?

   a) Cover your monitor with an anti-glare filter

   b) Password protect the data

   c) Take your computer with you when you leave your desk

   d) Never leave your desk

3. What is the name for different levels of access given to different users?

   a) Log on rights

   b) Password rights

   c) Data rights

   d) Access rights

4. What is the difference between a bug and a virus?

   a) A bug is a virus that only affects mainframe computers

   b) A bug is a virus that is not very serious

   c) A bug is an error in software code but a virus is malicious programming code

   d) A bug is malicious programming code but a virus is an error in software code

5. What is the name for a virus that disguises itself as something else, so you would be tempted to open it?

   a) A harpy

   b) A Trojan horse

   c) A Minotaur

   d) A gorgon

6. What should you use to help protect your computer against viruses?

   a)   Desktop publishing software

   b)   Graphics handling software

   c)   Database software

   d)   Anti-virus software

7. When was the Data Protection Act made law in the UK?

   a)   1980

   b)   1991

   c)   1998

   d)   2003

Exercise 1.16

1. Which is currently the most common way for a virus to enter your computer?

   a)   Via a borrowed floppy disk

   b)   Via e-mail or the Internet

   c)   Via a borrowed DVD

   d)   Via a borrowed CD

2. Anti-virus software is only useful if you:

   a)   Install the version recommended by your IT department

   b)   Run a scan for viruses every day

   c)   Update it regularly

   d)   Never borrow disks from anyone

3. Which of the following are subject to copyright legislation?

   a) A published book

   b) A music CD

   c) Software

   d) All of the above

4. What is the name for software that is provided free of charge or licensing fee?

   a) Freeware

   b) Shareware

   c) Hardware

   d) Software

5. What is the name for software provided for limited free evaluation before you buy it?

   a) Freeware

   b) Shareware

   c) Hardware

   d) Software

6. Which act governs the use and holding of personal data?

   a) The Health and Safety at Work Act

   b) The Criminal Justice Act

   c) The Data Protection Act

   d) The Personal Data Act

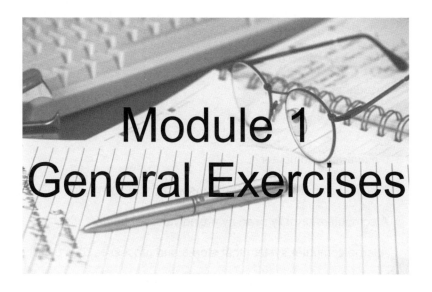

The following revision exercises can involve processes from any part of the ECDL/ICDL Syllabus 4 Module 1: Basic Concepts of I.T.

Exercise 1.17

1. What is the name for any external equipment attached to a computer?

   a) A modem

   b) A peripheral device

   c) A scanner

   d) A network

2. What is a mainframe computer?

   a) A small computer that can be transported in a carry case

   b) A computer normally used by an individual at home

   c) A large computer system that stores and processes data centrally

   d) A computer that can be held in the palm of a hand

3. A higher resolution on a monitor means:

   a) A poorer quality picture

   b) Better sound

   c) A colour display instead of black and white

   d) A better quality picture

4. What is "clock speed"?

   a) The speed of a computer's starting up process

   b) The speed at which a central processing unit can process information

   c) The amount of time gained by a computer's clock during the year

   d) The time it takes a user to change the date and time on their computer

Revision Series
© CiA Training Ltd 2005

5.   A scanner is (there may be more than one correct answer):

   a)   An input device

   b)   A peripheral

   c)   An output device

   d)   A gaming device

6.   Which of the following has the most storage space for electronic data?

   a)   A floppy disk

   b)   A 60 gigabyte hard drive

   c)   A CD

   d)   A filing cabinet

7.   How might you become aware that your computer's performance is deteriorating?

   a)   The screen turns green

   b)   Smoke is belching out of the back

   c)   It is becoming slower to perform tasks

   d)   It won't let you log on

8.   What is the general name for software programs such as spreadsheets, word processors, games, etc?

   a)   Utilities

   b)   Documents

   c)   Applications

   d)   Files

9. What type of person writes computer software programs?

   a) A systems analyser

   b) An administrator

   c) A technician

   d) A programmer

10. What type of file can be shared across a network?

    a) Any type of file

    b) Graphics files only

    c) Databases only

    d) Word processed documents only

11. What is a client/server network?

    a) Core data is stored on a central server accessed by individual workstations

    b) Core data, stored on a central server, which may only be accessed by clients of the company

    c) Two or more computers connected together

    d) Ten or more computers connected together

12. What is an ISP?

    a) Important Server Protector

    b) Internet Service Provider

    c) Information Services Portal

    d) Internet Server Protocol

13. What is a web browser?

    a)   Someone who spends a lot of time on the Internet

    b)   Someone with an interest in spiders

    c)   Software that allows you to send e-mail

    d)   Software that allows you to browse the World Wide Web

14. What is the name for an "internal Internet"?

    a)   An intranet

    b)   An extranet

    c)   An Ethernet

    d)   An internal net

15. Which of the following is a <u>disadvantage</u> of distance learning?

    a)   No travelling involved

    b)   You can learn at your own pace

    c)   Study at convenient times

    d)   No face to face interaction with others

16. Which of the following is an <u>advantage</u> of teleworking?

    a)   Lack of face to face interaction

    b)   Allows you to have a flexible schedule

    c)   Need to have more self discipline

    d)   You may start to feel isolated

17. What is the term for buying and selling goods and services online?

    a)   e-selling

    b)   e-shopping

    c)   e-commerce

    d)   e-trading

18. Which of the following is a common injury in an IT environment?

    a)   Cuts and bruises

    b)   Swollen fingers

    c)   Eye strain

    d)   Chronic boredom

19. Which of the following would make the most effective password?

    a)   Your first name

    b)   Your date of birth

    c)   A random mixture of letters and numbers

    d)   Your dog's name

20. What is an End User Agreement in relation to software?

    a)   It states who is allowed to use the software

    b)   It states who is allowed to install the software

    c)   It states exactly what a user is allowed to do with the software

    d)   It states how many people may use the software

Exercise 1.18

1. Which type of computer would not be suitable for home use?

    a)   PC

    b)   Laptop

    c)   PDA

    d)   Mainframe

2. Which of the following is not a peripheral?

    a)   VDU

    b)   Scanner

    c)   Plotter

    d)   CPU

3. Which of the following is a measure of computer speed?

    a)   MHz

    b)   KB

    c)   DPI

    d)   MPH

4. What type of memory cannot be altered?

    a)   RAM

    b)   ROM

    c)   Flash

    d)   Virtual

5. Which of the following sizes is the smallest?

    a)   Bit

    b)   Kilobyte

    c)   Gigabyte

    d)   Terabyte

6. Which of the following does affect computer speed (there may be more than one correct answer)?

    a)   Amount of RAM

    b)   Speed of CPU

    c)   Screen resolution

    d)   Number of applications running

7. What does GUI stand for?

    a)   Graphical Unit Interface

    b)   Graphical Update Interrupt

    c)   Graphical User Interface

    d)   Gradual Universal Interface

8. Which of the following is an operating system?

    a)   *Linux*

    b)   *Word*

    c)   *Notepad*

    d)   *Windows Explorer*

Revision Series
© CiA Training Ltd 2005

9. Which of the following office applications is used to open spreadsheets?

   a)   *Access*

   b)   *FrontPage*

   c)   *Outlook*

   d)   *Excel*

10. Which stage of system development checks for bugs?

   a)   Analysis

   b)   Programming

   c)   Testing

   d)   Documentation

11. Which of the following type of telecommunication is the quickest?

   a)   PSTN

   b)   ISDN

   c)   MODEM

   d)   ADSL

12. Which of these websites is not a search engine?

   a)   Google

   b)   Yahoo

   c)   Amazon

   d)   AltaVista

13. Which of the following is most suitable to use to send messages?

   a)   Email

   b)   Search engine

   c)   Web page

   d)   ISP

14. Which of these services can be categorized as e-commerce?

   a)   Providing Internet access

   b)   Selling books online

   c)   Delivering e-mail

   d)   Playing games online

15. Which of the following may be caused by poor ergonomics (there may be more than one correct answer)?

   a)   RSI

   b)   Increased performance

   c)   Eye strain

   d)   Computer running slower

16. What is a collection of computers connected together called?

   a)   A mainframe

   b)   A network

   c)   A CPU

   d)   ADSL

17. What does the term "Backing Up" mean?

    a)   Checking computer for viruses

    b)   Formatting a computer

    c)   Entering a username and password

    d)   Making a copy of important information

18. What may a user have to do to access secure data?

    a)   Check computer for viruses

    b)   Format a computer

    c)   Enter a username and password

    d)   Make copy of important information

19. Which of the following are classed as viruses (there may be more than one correct answer)?

    a)   Trojan

    b)   E-mail attachment

    c)   Worm

    d)   Macro

20. What can be used to ensure legitimate software belongs to the person installing it?

    a)   License agreement

    b)   Product ID

    c)   Data Protection Act

    d)   Trial period

Exercise 1.19

1. Which type of computer would a large company, rather than a home user, typically use?

   a)   PC

   b)   Laptop

   c)   PDA

   d)   Mainframe

2. What type of device is a touch screen?

   a)   An input and output device

   b)   An input device

   c)   An output device

   d)   A hardware device

3. Which of the following is a measure of hard disk size?

   a)   MHz

   b)   GB

   c)   DPI

   d)   MPH

4. Which of the following devices are input devices (there may be more than one correct answer)?

   a)   Monitor

   b)   Scanner

   c)   Microphone

   d)   Speaker

5. Which of the following sizes is the largest?

    a)   Bit

    b)   Kilobyte

    c)   Gigabyte

    d)   Terabyte

6. Which of the following does not affect computer speed?

    a)   Amount of RAM

    b)   Speed of CPU

    c)   Monitor size

    d)   Number of applications running

7. What does CPU stand for?

    a)   Central Prototype Unit

    b)   Concurrent Parallel Unit

    c)   Convex Picture Utensil

    d)   Central Processing Unit

8. Which of the following is <u>not</u> an operating system (there may be more than one correct answer)?

    a)   *Linux*

    b)   *Word*

    c)   *Notepad*

    d)   *Windows*

9.   Which of the following office applications is used to open databases?

    a)   *Access*

    b)   *FrontPage*

    c)   *Outlook*

    d)   *Excel*

10. Which stage of system development decides on the design?

    a)   Analysis

    b)   Programming

    c)   Testing

    d)   Documentation

11. Which of the following type of telecommunication is the slowest?

    a)   PSTN

    b)   ISDN

    c)   MODEM

    d)   ADSL

12. Which of these websites is a search engine?

    a)   Google

    b)   Microsoft

    c)   Amazon

    d)   NASA

13. Which of the following provides access to the Internet?

    a)   Email

    b)   Search engine

    c)   Web page

    d)   ISP

14. Which term describes the process of a computer starting up?

    a)   Antivirus

    b)   Defragment

    c)   Boot up

    d)   Application

15. Which of the following may <u>not</u> be carried out while using a spreadsheet application?

    a)   Typing text

    b)   Formatting data

    c)   Creating graphs

    d)   Creating slide shows

16. Which of the following is a type of computer connection?

    a)   A mainframe

    b)   A network

    c)   A CPU

    d)   ADSL

17. What would you use an antivirus application for?

    a)   Checking a computer for viruses

    b)   Formatting a computer

    c)   Entering a username and password

    d)   Making a copy of important information

18. Which of the following can be described as a network of computers?

    a)   Internet

    b)   Intranet

    c)   Extranet

    d)   World Wide Web

19. Which of the following are ways to help the environment (there may be more than one correct answer)?

    a)   Recycling waste paper

    b)   Using sleep/power off modes

    c)   Turning the heating down

    d)   Using wrist pads

20. How does shareware differ from freeware?

    a)   It has a license agreement

    b)   It is used for free

    c)   It is covered by the Data Protection Act

    d)   It has a trial period

Exercise 1.20

1. Which will typically use the most disk space and memory?

    a)   Photo image

    b)   Text file

    c)   A database

    d)   A game

2. Which of the following is an output device?

    a)   Mouse

    b)   Scanner

    c)   Plotter

    d)   CPU

3. What does OCR stand for?

    a)   Optimized concurrent register

    b)   Optical character recognition

    c)   Open computer rack

    d)   Overloaded computer rate

4. Which of the following affects quality of the picture on a VDU?

    a)   Number of applications running

    b)   Amount of RAM

    c)   Screen size

    d)   Number of speakers

Revision Exercises

5. Which of the following has the greatest storage capacity?

    a)   Floppy disk

    b)   Zip disk

    c)   CD

    d)   DVD

6. Which of the following statements describes a LAN?

    a)   Computers linked together in close proximity to each other

    b)   A network where core data is stored on a central computer

    c)   Computers linked together over large distances

    d)   The component needed to connect to the Internet

7. What does WAN stand for?

    a)   Wide Area Network

    b)   Working Annex Neuron

    c)   Wide Access Network

    d)   Windows Architecture Node

8. Which of the following are applications (there may be more than one correct answer)?

    a)   *Linux*

    b)   *Word*

    c)   *Notepad*

    d)   *Windows*

Revision Series
© CiA Training Ltd 2005

9. Which of the following can be described as a server?

    a)   A network computer

    b)   A PDA

    c)   A laptop

    d)   An *Excel* file

10. Which stage is typically not a part of system development?

    a)   Analysis

    b)   Programming

    c)   Testing

    d)   Reverse Engineering

11. Which of the following is a measure of transfer rate?

    a)   BPS

    b)   ISDN

    c)   ROM

    d)   ADSL

12. Which of these is an analogue Internet connection?

    a)   ADSL

    b)   PSTN

    c)   ISDN

    d)   POST

13. Which of the following displays information on the World-Wide Web?

   a)   E-mail

   b)   Search engine

   c)   Web page

   d)   ISP

14. Which term is another name for a computer program?

   a)   Antivirus

   b)   Defragment

   c)   Boot up

   d)   Application

15. In relation to viruses, what is a payload?

   a)   A virus that replicates itself within a system

   b)   The action the virus carries out

   c)   A virus that has been added to an executable file

   d)   A virus disguised as a file a user would open

16. Which type of file can be copyrighted (there may be more than one correct answer)?

   a)   An image file

   b)   An audio file

   c)   A text file

   d)   A video file

Revision Series
© CiA Training Ltd 2005

17. Which of the following is enforced by the Data Protection Act?

    a)   Data will be accurate and, where necessary, kept up to date

    b)   Data will be held for as long as possible

    c)   Data will not be protected

    d)   Data shall be gathered by all means possible

18. What should be done with back up data (choose more than one)?

    a)   Kept off site

    b)   Kept secure

    c)   Discarded when a new back up is made

    d)   Kept near the computer it was taken from

19. What can e-mail be used for (choose more than one)?

    a)   Inter-office communication

    b)   Sending files to correspondents

    c)   Protecting files

    d)   Saving power

20. What can be used to describe freeware (there may be more than one correct answer)?

    a)   It has a license agreement

    b)   It can be used for free

    c)   It is exempt from copyright protection legislation

    d)   It has a trial period

Revision Exercises

Exercise 1.21

1. Which of the following computers is the smallest?

    a)   Laptop

    b)   PC

    c)   Mainframe

    d)   PDA

2. Which of the following is <u>not</u> a peripheral?

    a)   Hard Drive

    b)   Monitor

    c)   Printer

    d)   Mouse

3. Which of the following allows a CD to be read?

    a)   Plotter

    b)   Scanner

    c)   CPU

    d)   CD-ROM Drive

4. Applications and utilities are examples of what?

    a)   Hardware

    b)   Speakers

    c)   Operating systems

    d)   Software

5. Which component controls the transfer of information between secondary and main memory?

   a) RAM

   b) CPU

   c) ROM

   d) PSU

6. What is voice recognition software used with?

   a) Microphone

   b) Speaker

   c) Printer

   d) Hard drive

7. Which of the following can be used to allow freehand drawing and writing to be entered into a PC?

   a) Scanner

   b) Plotter

   c) Digital camera

   d) Graphics tablet

8. Where can information be saved to (there may be more than one correct answer)?

   a) ROM

   b) CD

   c) Hard drive

   d) CPU

9. Which of the following actions is not recommended?

    a)   Backing up data

    b)   Virus checking

    c)   Formatting hard disks

    d)   Saving data to a hard disk

10. Which of the following types of memory loses all information it holds once it is turned off?

    a)   ROM

    b)   RAM

    c)   Flash

    d)   Virtual

11. When a collection of text and graphics is saved it can be called what?

    a)   File

    b)   Utility

    c)   Application

    d)   Antivirus

12. What uses icons, menus and windows to show the computer's facilities?

    a)   CPU

    b)   RAM

    c)   POST

    d)   GUI

13. What does DTP stand for?

    a)   Double transport protocol

    b)   Desktop publishing

    c)   Durable traffic polling

    d)   Desktop printing

14. What are two computers connected together called?

    a)   A network

    b)   A mainframe

    c)   A server

    d)   A laptop

15. What does WWW stand for?

    a)   World- Wide Web

    b)   World-wide working week

    c)   Web wiring weight

    d)   Web wiring wattage

16. For safety, what should you do to an e-mail attachment before opening it?

    a)   Save it

    b)   Nothing, just open it

    c)   Virus scan it

    d)   Format it

17. Which of the following is <u>not</u> an advantage of distance learning for the student?

 a) Learn at own pace

 b) No travelling involved

 c) More control over learning process

 d) Reduces company space requirements

18. Which of the following is <u>not</u> an advantage of computer systems?

 a) Cannot use initiative

 b) Automation of repetitive tasks

 c) Accurate control of machines

 d) Fast data manipulation

19. Which of the following leads to good ergonomics (there may be more than one correct answer)?

 a) Provision of mouse mat

 b) Suitably positioned keyboard

 c) Anti glare screen for monitor

 d) Turning computer to standby mode

20. What can an antivirus program do to a virus (there may be more than one correct answer)?

 a) Disinfect

 b) Format

 c) Quarantine

 d) Edit

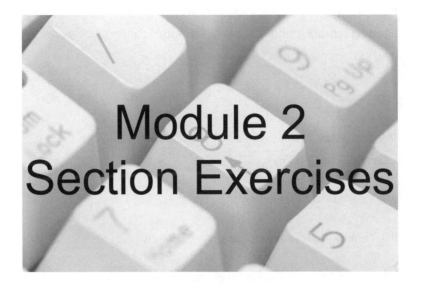

Module 2
Section Exercises

The following revision exercises are divided into sections, each targeted at specific elements of the ECDL/ICDL Syllabus 4 Module 2: Using the Computer and Managing Files. The individual sections are an exact match for the sections in the ECDL/ICDL Syllabus 4 Training Guides from CiA Training, making the guides an ideal reference source for anyone working through these exercises.

Getting Started

These exercises include topics taken from the following list: starting, restarting and closing down the computer, identifying parts of a window, understanding the **Start** menu and **Taskbar**, recognising, creating and arranging **Desktop** icons, opening, resizing and closing windows, viewing system properties and using **Help**.

Exercise 2.1

1. With the computer already switched on, move the mouse over the **Start** button. What does the **ToolTip** say?

2. Where is the **Taskbar** located on the screen?

3. Drag the **Taskbar** to three times its original height.

4. Click on the **Start** button and open any program.

5. Open another program.

6. Switch between the two programs using the **Taskbar**.

7. Close both applications and return the **Taskbar** to its original height.

8. Open **My Computer**.

9. Resize the window using the mouse pointer until the scroll bars can be seen.

10. Move the window to the bottom right of the screen.

11. Use the scroll bars to see the items at the bottom of the window.

12. Close **My Computer** and restart the computer.

Exercise 2.2

1. Begin this exercise with the computer switched off. Turn on the computer and log in if required.

2. View the **System Properties**.

3. View the **Device Manager**.

4. Arrange the open windows around the screen and increase the size of the **Device Manager** dialog box.

5. Close any open windows.

6. Use **Help** to find information about arranging **Desktop** icons.

7. Close **Help** and move all of the **Desktop** icons into a large circle.

8. Arrange the icons **by Name**.

9. Restart the computer while it is running.

10. Use the **Start Menu** to find the *Calculator* program (usually within the **Accessories** folder.)

11. Click on the **Calculator** text to open it and move it to the top left of the screen.

12. Open another **Calculator** in the same way.

13. Position this window next to the first.

14. Continue until the whole screen is covered.

15. Close all **Calculators**.

Managing Files

These exercises include topics taken from the following list: understanding drives, files and folders, understanding file types, formatting and backing up to a removable disk, copying, moving, renaming and deleting files and folders, creating folders, using the **Recycle Bin** and searching for files and folders.

Exercise 2.3

1. View the **Module 2 Data** folder.

2. Copy the **Award Certificate** *Publisher* file.

3. Paste the file in the same location.

4. Rename the copied file as **Great Idea Award**.

5. In **Details** view, sort the folder by **Type**.

6. How many different file types are there in this folder?

7. Use the mouse and keyboard to select **Countries.htm**, **Dinosaur.jpg** and **Formulas.xls**.

8. View the properties of these three files to see the total size. What is it?

9. Select all <u>files</u> except **CD Collection.mdb**, what is the combined size of the selected files?

10. Search the **Module 2 Data** folder for **Egypt** as a **word or phrase within a file**. How many files are found?

Exercise 2.4

1. Format a floppy disk.

2. Copy all of the files from the **Module 2 Data** folder to the floppy disk as backup.

3. Create a new folder called **Microsoft** in the **Module 2 Data** folder.

4. Copy each of the files with the word *Microsoft* in the file type to this new folder. How many files are there?

5. Look at the contents of the new folder, then create a subfolder for each of the different programs used, e.g. *Word, Excel*. How many subfolders are there?

6. Move the files into the correct folders.

7. Use the **Type of file** drop down list in **More advanced options** in the **Search** dialog box to list all of the **folders** in the **Microsoft** folder.

   Note: *In Windows 2000, use the **Type** drop down list in **Search Options**.*

8. From this list delete the **PowerPoint** folder.

9. Close the **Search** dialog box and check that the folder has been deleted.

10. From the **Recycle Bin** restore the folder.

Print Management

These exercises include topics taken from the following list: selecting a printer, setting a default printer, adding a new printer, viewing a print job and controlling print jobs.

Exercise 2.5

1. Open the **Printers and Faxes** window (**Printer** window in *Windows 2000*).

2.   View the properties of the default printer.

3.   How many tabs appear along the top of this dialog box?

4.   View the **print queue** of the default printer.

5.   Pause the printing for this printer.

6.   Leave the **print queue** open and locate the **CiA Training Ltd** document.

7.   Right click on this file and select **Print**.

8.   View the **print queue**.

9.   Cancel the *Word* document print job and resume the printing for this printer.

Exercise 2.6

1.   Open the **Printers and Faxes** window (**Printer** window in *Windows 2000*).

2.   What feature helps with adding a new printer?

3.   Use the **Help** section in the **Printers and Faxes** window to find information on how to **Print a test page**.

4.   Close the **Help** dialog box.

5.   View the **Properties** of the default printer.

6.   What is the name of the second tab along the top of the dialog box.

7.   Close the **Printer Properties** dialog box and the **Printers and Faxes** window.

Running Applications

These exercises include topics taken from the following list: starting and closing an application, entering text, saving and printing information, capturing screen images, installing and removing applications, switching between applications and creating and using **Desktop** items.

Exercise 2.7

1. Open the *WordPad* program.

2. What are the lines of buttons near the top of the screen called?

3. Which options are available in the **Format** menu?

4. Open the *Calculator* program.

5. Switch between the open windows until *WordPad* can be seen again.

6. Enter the following text:

   This is a test document which will be stored on the computer.

7. Change the word **stored** to **saved**.

8. Save the file as **WordPad** in the **Module 2 Data** folder.

9. Switch back to the *Calculator* and take a **Screen Shot**.

10. Switch back to *WordPad*, create a new document, and paste the image into it.

11. Change the layout to **Landscape**.

12. Reduce the size of the image so it fits on the page.

13. Save the document as **Calculator** in the same place as the **WordPad** file.

14. Close the *Wordpad* and *Calculator* programs.

Exercise 2.8

1. Display the **Add or Remove Programs** dialog box and select one of the programs.

2. Which button would delete an application?

3. Close the dialog box.

4. Create a **Desktop** shortcut for the *WordPad* application.

5. Rename the shortcut **Double click to open WordPad**.

6. Create a **Desktop** shortcut for the **Dinosaur.jpg** file in the **Module 2 Data** folder.

7. Rename the shortcut **Double click to open the Dinosaur**.

8. Locate the program **NotePad.exe** and add it to the **Start** menu. The program should be found in **C:\Windows\system32** or **C:\Windows**

9. Test all 3 shortcuts, then delete each one.

Using Compress

These exercises include topics taken from the following list: understanding file compression, compressing files and extracting compressed files.

Exercise 2.9

1. Unzip the file **Secret.zip** into the same location as the zip file is stored.

Revision Series
© CiA Training Ltd 2005

2.   Double click on the unzipped file to open it.

3.   Which program is used to open the file?

4.   What is the **Secret Number**?

5.   Close the file.

6.   What is the size of the zipped file?

7.   What is the size of the unzipped file?

8.   Delete the zipped file.

9.   Zip the file again. Is the zipped file the same size as before?

Exercise 2.10

1.   What is the size of the **Rainbow.tif** file?

2.   What is the size of the **Flower.tif** file?

3.   These files are to be compressed together into a single file. What kind of program will achieve this?

4.   Using this program, create a new folder called **Zipped** with a file called **Images** for the files to be compressed into.

5.   Add the 2 files and close the program.

6.   What is the size of the **Images.zip** file?

7.   Copy this file on to a floppy disk.

Virus Control

These exercises include topics taken from the following list: Understanding viruses, understanding virus transmission, understanding virus protection and using virus protection applications.

Exercise 2.11

1. What is a virus?

2. Do viruses always cause the same damage?

3. Is it possible to get a virus without an Internet connection?

4. Name 3 ways a virus can be transmitted to your computer.

5. What is the most common way of receiving a virus?

6. Which two modes does virus protection software have?

Exercise 2.12

1. Use your virus protection software to check the **Module 2 Data** folder for viruses.

2. What kind of damage can viruses cause?

3. Explain the process of **disinfecting** viruses.

4. What does a continuously running **shield** do?

5. What is the problem with comparing the code of the system to a list of known viruses?

6. How are protection applications usually updated?

Revision Series
© CiA Training Ltd 2005

Control Panel

These exercises include topics taken from the following list: changing date and time, controlling the background, choosing the screen saver, selecting settings and effects and controlling sound and multimedia.

2

Exercise 2.13

1. Display the **Date and Time Properties** dialog box.

2. Ensure the date and time are correct. Make any changes if required.

3. Change the **Time Zone** to see the effect on the map.

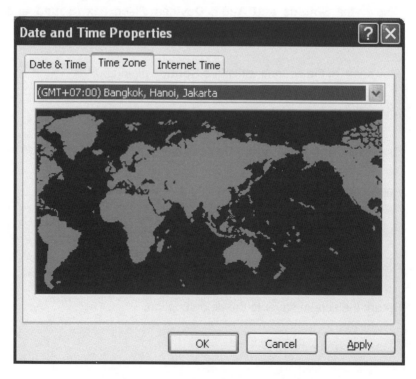

4. Ensure the correct **Time Zone** is selected before leaving the dialog box.

5.   View the **Display** dialog box.

6.   Change the **Background** image.

7.   Add a **Marquee Screen Saver** and alter the **Settings** to text of your choice.

8.   **Preview** the **Screen Saver** to check the writing and speed are as desired.

9.   Return the display to its original settings by selecting **None** for **Background** and **Screen Saver**.

Exercise 2.14

1.   Display the **Sounds and Audio Devices** dialog box (**Sound and Multimedia** in *Windows 2000*).

2.   Play some of the sounds within the **Sounds** dialog box.

3.   Adjust the **Volume** slider then repeat playing the sounds.

4.   Close the **Sound and Audio Devices** dialog box.

5.   Apply a **Marquee** screen saver using your name as the text.

6.   Adjust the font, size, colour and speed of the text.

7.   Preview the screen saver.

8.   Return the screen saver to the default option.

9.   Close all open windows.

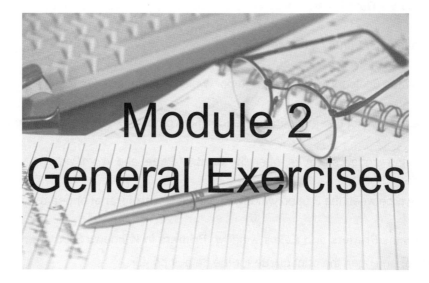

The following revision exercises can involve processes from any part of the ECDL/ICDL Syllabus 4 Module 2: Using the Computer and Managing Files.

Exercise 2.15

1. View the contents of the **General Exercises** folder, which is found within the **Module 2 Data** folder.

2. Rename the **Films** folder **Movies**.

3. Copy the 6 folders in the **Action** folder, which is in the **Movies** folder.

4. Paste a copy of these folders into each of the other 3 folders in the **Movies** folder.

5. With the window still open, open the **Control Panel** and *WordPad*.

6. Switch between the 3 open windows until the **Control Panel** appears.

7. Open the **Printers and Faxes** window (**Printers** in *Windows 2000*) from the **Control Panel** and open the print queue for the default printer.

8. Choose to **Pause Printing**.

9. Switch back to **WordPad**.

10. Type: **This is a test document and should not print until the printer is not paused!**

11. Save the document as **Printing** in the **Word Processing** folder of the **Documents** folder.

12. Select **Print**.

13. Resume the printing so that the document is printed.

14. Close all open windows.

15. Create a shortcut in the **Start** menu to the folder **Comedy** within the **Movies** folder.

16. View the **Start Menu** and rename the shortcut **Comedy Movies**.

17. Click on the shortcut to view the subfolders.

18. Delete the shortcut.

Exercise 2.16

1. Copy all of these files from the original data folder to the appropriate subfolder within the **Documents** folder:

> *Access* files → **Databases** folder
>
> *Excel* files → **Spreadsheets** folder
>
> *FrontPage* files → **Web Pages** folder
>
> *PowerPoint* files → **Presentations** folder
>
> *Publisher* files→ **Desk Top Publishing** folder (create a new folder)
>
> *Word* files → **Word Processing** folder

2. Rename the **Desk Top Publishing** folder as **DTP**.

3. What is the size of the **Spreadsheets** folder?

4. Format a floppy disk.

5. Use file compression software to compress the whole **Module 2 Data** folder on to the floppy disk (if you have completed Exercise 2.7, you may have to delete the **Calculator.rtf** file before attempting the compression).

6. Check the size of the file on the floppy disk and compare this to the size of the folder on the computer.

7.   Create a print screen showing the floppy disk zipped folder.

8.   Open *WordPad* and select **Edit | Paste**.

9.   Resize the image to fit on a single **Landscape** screen.

10. Save the file as **Zipped Folder** into the **Word Processing** folder.

11. Create a **Desktop** icon for this file.

12. Rename the shortcut **Zipped Pic**.

13. Open the file via the shortcut.

14. Delete the shortcut.

15. Restore the shortcut.

Exercise 2.17

1.   Open the **Control Panel**.

2.   Display the **Date and Time Properties** dialog box.

3.   Ensure that the correct date and time are displayed and the correct time zone is specified.

4.   Close this dialog box and open the **Display Properties** dialog box.

5.   Apply a **Marquee Screen Saver** with the text **This is my screensaver**.

6.   Alter the **Speed** of the marquee to slow and the **Background Color** to blue.

7.   Format the text used as **Red, Arial, 36 point**.

8. **Preview** the screensaver and apply the changes.

9. Change the **Desktop** background and apply the changes.

10. Close all windows to view the new **Desktop**.

11. Return the display to its original settings.

12. Open *WordPad*, *Calculator* and *Paint*.

13. Resize and position these windows so all can be seen fully on screen.

14. Create a print screen of these three windows.

15. Paste the screen into *WordPad* and resize the image to fit on a single page.

16. Save the file as **3 screens** in **My Documents**.

17. Move this file from **My Documents** to the **Word Processing** folder.

18. Rename the file as **3 Print Screens**.

19. Search for a file with **3** in the title to locate the **3 Print Screens** again.

20. Delete the file.

21. Restore the file and create a **Start** menu shortcut for it.

22. Delete the shortcut.

Revision Exercises

Exercise 2.18

1. Search for a file containing the text **ICDL** within the **Module 2 Data** folder.

2. The **International CiA Training Ltd** file should be found. Note where the file is stored.

3. Close the **Search** window.

4. Create a new folder within the **Documents** folder called **Information**.

5. Copy the **International CiA Training Ltd** file into this new folder.

6. In the new folder, rename the file as **CiA Training International Info**.

7. Open a dialog box from the **Control Panel** which will allow you to control the sounds which are produced by your computer.

8. Click the **Sounds** tab and click once on the **Close Program** text within the **Windows** group.

9. A sound is to be added which will be heard when a program is closed.

10. Choose one of the available sounds and click **Play Sound** to preview the sound.

11. Save the **Sound scheme** as **Test**.

12. Set the slider for volume control midway between **Low** and **High**.

13. Close the **Control Panel** then open *WordPad*.

14. Close *WordPad* to hear the new sound chosen.

15. Remove the sound from the **Close Program** operation and delete the **Test** scheme.

Exercise 2.19

1. Open the **Search** function.

2. Search for any files or folders with the text **pic** as part of the filename. Ensure that only the supplied data folder and its subfolders are being searched.

3. Restrict the search to files of not more than **1Mb** (**Medium**).

4. Select the type of file as **WinZip File** (or **Compressed (zipped) Folder**) and ensure all subfolders are searched.

5. The search should produce a single result. What is the filename?

6. Take note of the folder containing the file and close the **Search Results** dialog box.

7. Find the file and extract it to the same folder.

8. Use the *Calculator* to find the difference in size between the 2 files.

9. Delete the zipped file.

10. Create a **Desktop** shortcut for the unzipped file.

11. Close all open windows.

12. Double click on the new shortcut to ensure it opens the correct picture.

13. Close the program.

14. Rearrange all of the **Desktop** icons to surround the new shortcut.

15. Arrange the **Desktop** icons by **Size**.

16. Delete the shortcut.

17. Compress the file and save it to a floppy disk as **Image.zip**.

18. Delete the unzipped file.

19. Check the floppy disk for viruses.

20. Uncompress the file into the same folder it was in originally.

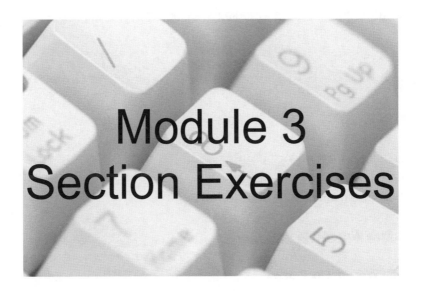

**Module 3
Section Exercises**

3

The following revision exercises are divided into sections, each targeted at specific elements of the ECDL/ICDL Syllabus 4 Module 3: Word Processing. The individual sections are an exact match for the sections in the ECDL/ICDL Syllabus 4 Training Guides from CiA Training, making the guides an ideal reference source for anyone working through these exercises.

Getting Started

These exercises include topics taken from the following list: starting *Word*, recognising the screen layout, using the menus and toolbars, using help and the office assistant, exiting *Word*.

Exercise 3.1

1. Start *Word*.

2. Resize the **Formatting** toolbar.

3. Use help to find information on **Printing**.

4. Display the **WordArt** toolbar.

5. Hide the **WordArt** toolbar.

6. Which one of the following is <u>not</u> the name of a toolbar in *Word*?

    a)   Frames

    b)   Picture

    c)   Drawing

    d)   Image

7. When the mouse pointer is hovering over a toolbar button what is displayed?

8. True or false? Toolbars are always displayed along the top of the window, under the Menu Bar.

9. Display the complete **Tools** menu. How many options are ghosted?

10. Exit *Word*.

Exercise 3.2

1. Start *Word*.

2. Use the **Office Assistant** to find information on **Tabs**.

3. Which commands will display a list of all the available toolbars?

4. Which menu contains the **Arrange All** option?

5. Select **Tools | Options**. What is the title of the resulting dialog box?

6. Can this dialog box be resized?

7. Click **Cancel** on the dialog box to remove it.

8. Get help on **Formatting**.

9. Exit *Word*.

Documents

These exercises include topics taken from the following list: entering text, working in different views, opening, saving and closing documents, saving a document in web page format, saving documents in other formats.

Exercise 3.3

1. Start *Word*.

2. Type a few sentences about yourself.

3. Select **File | Close**. What message is displayed?

4. Click **Cancel** in the message box to cancel the close process.

5. Save the document as **Personal**. What extension is added by default to a saved document in *Word*?

6. Close the document.

7. Open the document **Rich** from the supplied data files.

8. Press <**Enter**> at the end of the text and type an extra line:

   It is therefore a useful format for e-mail messages.

9. Save the document as a **Rich Text Format** file with the same name. What file extension is added?

10. Close the document.

Exercise 3.4

1. Start a new document in *Word* and type some text about your hobbies.

2. Switch to **Outline View**.

3. Switch to **Web layout view**.

4. Use a specific command to save the page as a web page with the name **Hobbies**. What file extension is added by default?

5. Close the document and open the document **Plain** from the supplied data files.

6. Press <**Enter**> at the end of the text and type an extra line:

   Plain text files take up the least space of any text file type.

7. Save the document as a **Plain Text** file (or **Text Only** file in *Word 2000*) with the same name. What file extension is added?

8. A warning is displayed. Why is this? Click **OK** (or **Yes**) to accept the warning.

9. Close *Word*.

Editing Text

These exercises include topics taken from the following list: inserting and deleting text, selecting words and sentences, selecting lines and paragraphs, inserting special characters and symbols, using undo and redo, showing and hiding non printing characters, inserting and deleting soft carriage returns.

Exercise 3.5

1. Open the document **Gardens**.

2. Insert a formatting control in the heading, between **Toffington Gardens** and **Grand Opening** so that each part appears on a separate line but the whole title will still be considered as a single paragraph.

3. Use a toolbar button to display non printing characters. What is the symbol for the control added in the last step?

    a) ¶   b) ↵   c) ✳

4. Insert a paragraph break at the end of the first sentence.

5. Insert a blank line after this to separate it from the next paragraph.

6. Place the cursor in the last sentence of the third paragraph. What key combination will select the whole sentence?

7. Select the whole sentence and delete it.

8. Click the **Undo** button. What happens?

9. In the second paragraph, replace the word **estate** with **grounds**.

10. In the fifth paragraph, insert the word **relaxing** before the word **picnic.**

11. Save the document as **Gardens2** and close it.

Exercise 3.6

1. Open the document **Ballet**.

2. Replace the word **veteran** with **experienced** and the word **troupe** with **company**.

3. Insert a soft carriage return between the two sentences of the first paragraph.

4. Insert the registered symbol after **Barnacle Ballet Company**.

5. Insert the trademark symbol after **Duck Pond**.

6. Select the whole paragraph starting **All proceeds** and delete it.

7.   Insert the following three paragraphs of text at the end of the document:

> Not advisable for those of a nervous disposition
>
> ♪ Music by the accomplished composer Ivor Stringvesto
>
> ① For more information visit our web site

Note: *The symbols used can be found in the Webdings font.*

8.   Use a key press to select the entire document.

9.   Press the **q** key. What happens?

10. Click **Undo** to retrieve the document content.

11. Save the document as **Ballet2** and close it.

Printing

These exercises include topics taken from the following list: previewing a document, printing a document, printing parts of a document, and printing specific pages.

Exercise 3.7

1.   Open the document **Hall**.

2.   Select print preview.

3.   Make sure the display shows one page only.

4.   Make sure the **Magnifier** cursor is selected and click once on the page to enlarge it. What is the **Zoom** setting with the page enlarged?

5.   Click again to return to the previous magnification.

6. Change the view so that the preview shows both pages at once. What is the name of the button used to do this?

7. Close print preview.

8. Select the section of the document describing the house (with the sub-heading) and print a copy of this section only.

9. Close the document <u>without</u> saving.

Exercise 3.8

1. Open the document **Viruses**.

2. Select print preview.

3. Show multiple pages (**1x2** pages).

4. Change the **Zoom** value to **50%**.

5. Change the multiple display to **1x6** pages.

6. Close print preview and print a copy of page **2** of the document only.

7. Select print preview again, (**1x2** pages). Select **shrink to fit**. The document should now be all on one page.

8. Close print preview. How has the document been amended to fit on to one page?

9. Print one copy of the first paragraph of the document, including the item title.

10. Close the document <u>without</u> saving.

Formatting Text

These exercises include topics taken from the following list: underlining, emboldening and italicising text, changing fonts and text size, applying text effects, subscript and superscript, using the format painter, cutting, copying and pasting.

Exercise 3.9

1. Open the **LakeDistrict** document.

2. Change the font of the entire document to **Tahoma**.

3. Change the size of the title, **The English Lake District**, to **14pt**.

4. Change the title to upper case and **Bold**.

5. Select the first sub heading, **Rocks**, and format it as **Bold** and **Underlined**.

6. Change the colour of this sub heading to **dark green**.

7. Use a toolbar button to apply all this formatting to the other sub headings, **Glaciation** and **Civilisation**.

8. In the last section, italicise the first word in each of the last four paragraphs (**Agriculture**, **Forestry**, **Mining**, **Tourism**).

9. Change the font of the first paragraph of text to **Verdana** and apply formatting of **Italic** and a colour of **dark green**.

10. Use editing commands to move the entire first paragraph to the end of the document so that it becomes the last paragraph.

11. Save the document as **Lakes2** and close it.

Revision Exercises

Exercise 3.10

1. Start a blank *Word* document and type the following text:

   The British Banking System is now heavily committed to the use of computers in order to give a much faster and more effective service to the increasing number of people who now have bank accounts.

   The banks are making increasing use of cashpoint machines. These are special computer terminals, connected to the bank's computer, which allow customers to withdraw money and make use of other banking services outside of normal banking hours.

2. Format the entire document as **Century Gothic, 12pt**

3. Copy the text **British Banking System** and paste it as a title to the text.

4. Underline the title.

5. Make the text **British Banking System** in the first sentence italic and red.

6. Use the format painter to copy this formatting to the word **cashpoint**.

7. On a new line at the end of the document type the text **A ceiling**. Press the <**Tab**> key twice and type **B floor**.

8. Change the font size of the new line to **18pt**.

9. Format the words **ceiling** and **floor** as **Superscript** and **Subscript** respectively.

10. Change the colour of the whole line to **dark blue**.

11. Save the document as **Banks2** and close it.

Revision Series
© CiA Training Ltd 2005

Tools

These exercises include topics taken from the following list: checking spelling, hyphenating text, searching for text, replacing text, using the zoom control, and changing preferences.

Exercise 3.11

1. Open the document **Tours**.

2. Check the item for spelling mistakes.

3. Replace mistakes by making a choice from the suggestions.

4. **LearnersVille** is a name, not a spelling mistake. Ignore this.

5. Hyphenate the document automatically.

6. Add your name as the user name in the **User Information** for the document.

7. Replace all occurrences of the name Learnersville with the name of the town/city where you live.

8. Save the document as **Tours2** and close it.

Exercise 3.12

1. Open the document **Hall**.

2. Change the **Zoom** setting to **Whole Page**. What is a disadvantage of this view?

3. Change the **Zoom** setting to **Text Width**. What is a disadvantage of this view?

4.   Change the **Zoom** setting to **100%**.

5.   Check the document for spelling mistakes. Although there should be no actual mistakes, several names will be highlighted as unrecognised words. Which different names are highlighted? Ignore each one as it appears.

6.   Replace every occurrence of the word **house** in the document with the word **hall**. How many replacements are made?

7.   Check the preferences for the document and note down the default location for the saving and retrieval of normal documents.

8.   Close the document <u>without</u> saving.

Formatting Paragraphs

These exercises include topics taken from the following list: aligning text, indenting paragraphs, applying advanced indentation, applying bullets and numbers, changing line and paragraph spacing, applying and changing tab settings, changing tab alignment, and applying borders.

Exercise 3.13

1.   Open the document **LakeDistrict**.

2.   **Centre** align the title and make it **Bold**.

3.   Apply a left indentation of **1cm** to the whole of the first paragraph.

4.   Apply a left indentation of **1cm** to the first line <u>only</u> in each of the next 4 paragraphs.

5.   Select the whole document and apply a spacing of **6pt** to appear after every paragraph.

6. In the **Glaciation** section is a list of seven examples, starting with **Hanging Valleys**. Make this a bulleted list using any bullet character.

7. Apply an alignment of **Justified** to the bulleted list.

8. In the **Civilisation** section, make the last four paragraphs into a list numbered **1. 2. 3.** and **4**.

9. Increase the line spacing for the first paragraph of the document to **1.5** lines.

10. Add a **1pt shadow** border to the same paragraph.

11. Save the document as **Lakes3** and close it.

Exercise 3.14

1. Create a blank document in *Word*.

2. Set left aligned tab stops at positions **4cm** and **8cm**.

3. Enter the text **Name Department Telephone** using the **Tab** key so that the word **Department** lines up with the first tab stop and **Telephone** lines up with the second. Press <**Enter**> to end the line.

4. On the next line enter the text **John Smith Admin 432** using the **Tab** key so that **Admin** lines up under **Department** and **432** lines up under **Telephone**.

5. Enter the following lines in the same manner:

    Tracy Jones   Sales   135

    Tariq Hussan   Admin   446

    Nina Kurpova   Sales   158

6. Change the line spacing to **Double** for the whole document.

7. Move the tab stop positions for the whole list to **6cm** and **13cm**.

8. Change the **13cm** tab to be **Right** aligned.

9. Change the **Right Indent** for the whole list to **1.24cm** (or set it to **14cm** on the ruler).

10. Apply a **1pt Box** border to the whole list.

11. Apply a shading of **Gray 10%** to the list.

12. Make the first line of the list **Bold**.

13. Save the document as **List2** and close it.

Multiple Documents

These exercises include topics taken from the following list: switching between open documents, cutting, copying and pasting between documents, applying headers and footers, and applying page numbering.

Exercise 3.15

1. Open the document **Gardens**, then open the document **Hall**.

2. Use a menu option to switch to the **Gardens** document again. Which menu is used?

3. Format the whole **Gardens** document as **Arial** font with **Double** line spacing.

4. At the end of the document leave a blank line then add the sentence:
   Visitors can also take a tour of the main Toffington Hall buildings.

5. Switch to the **Hall** document and copy the three paragraphs of text under the **House** subheading.

6. Switch back to the **Gardens** document and paste the text starting on a new line after the newly added sentence.

7. Make sure the newly added text has the same formatting as the previous paragraphs.

8. Enter your name as a text entry in the centre of the document Header.

9. Enter an automatic page number field in the centre of the document Footer.

10. Print a copy of the complete document.

11. Save the **Gardens** document as **Gardens3**, then close it.

12. Close the **Hall** document <u>without</u> saving.

Exercise 3.16

1. Create a new blank document.

2. Open the **LakeDistrict** document.

3. Copy the section on **Rocks** from the **LakeDistrict** document.

4. Switch to the blank document and paste the copied text.

5. Save the new document as **Rocks2**.

6. View the **Header** and insert the **Filename** of the document as an **Autotext** field on the left of the area.

7. View the **Footer** and using a single command, insert the **Author**, **Page Number** and **Date** as an **Autotext** field.

8. In which of the four main views, **Normal**, **Web Layout**, **Print Layout** and **Outline**, will the headers and footers be visible?

9. Print a copy of the **Rocks2** document.

10. Save the **Rocks2** document then close it.

11. Close the **LakeDistrict** document <u>without</u> saving.

Tables

These exercises include topics taken from the following list: inserting tables, entering text into tables, selecting cells, changing column width, inserting and deleting cells, inserting rows and columns, and applying borders.

Exercise 3.17

1. Open a new blank document and insert a table of 4 columns and 7 rows.

2. Enter the following data into the table :

Name	Continent	Range	Height(m)
Everest	Asia	Himalayas	8850
Annapurna	Asia	Himalayas	8091
Acongagua	South America	Andes	6962
Mount McKinley	North America	Alaskan	6194
Kilimanjaro	Africa	Volcano	5895
Mont Blanc	Europe	Alps	4807

3. Format all the table content as **Arial 12pt** and make sure all borders are displayed.

4. Insert a new column on the right of the table with a heading of **First Ascent**.

5. Add data **1953**, **1950**, **1897**, **1913**, **1889**, **1786** down the column.

6. Adjust the width of the columns if necessary so that all data is displayed and each cell only requires a single line.

7. Format the first row content as **Bold** and **Centred**.

8. Apply a **1½ pt** box border to the first row.

9. Apply a **Gray-20%** shading to the first row.

10. Apply a shading of **palest green** to the remaining cells of the table.

11. Save the document as **Mountains** and close it.

Exercise 3.18

1. Start a new blank document in *Word* and enter a centred title of **Maintenance Log**.

2. Insert a table of 2 columns and 4 rows.

3. Type the column headers **Date** and **Name**.

4. Insert a new column after **Name** and add the header **Action Taken**.

5. Specify the three column widths as **3cm**, **4cm** and **7cm** respectively.

6. Enter the following information :

12/04/05	Jim Dawson	Door handle repaired in office 10a
16/08/05	Jim Dawson	Broken window in 1st floor break room replaced
23/08/05	Amy Madson	Broken chair in conference room 2 replaced

7. Widen the **Action Taken** column as required so that all the data in each row is displayed and shown on a single line.

8. Set the height of all rows to be **0.7**.

9. Remove all borders and add a **1½pt** box border around the whole table.

10. Insert a few blank lines after the table.

11. Create the following table. The text is all **Arial 12pt bold** except **Total** which is **Arial 14pt bold**. The shading is all **Gray - 20%** except **Total** which is **Gray - 35%**. The cell to the right of **Total** has a **1½pt** border.

Weekly Time Sheet		
Employee		
	Hours Worked	**Signature**
Mon		
Tues		
Wed		
Thur		
Fri		
Total		

12. Save the document as **Log** and close it.

Document Manipulation

These exercises include topics taken from the following list: selecting paper size, changing page orientation, changing margins, inserting page breaks, and applying styles.

Exercise 3.19

1. Open the document **LakeDistrict**.

2. Change the **Left** and **Right** page margins to **4cm**.

3. Change the **Top** and **Bottom** page margins to **3cm**.

4. Set the orientation to **Landscape**.

5. Insert page breaks before the **Glaciation** and **Civilisation** subheadings.

6. Apply the style **Heading1** to the main title of the document.

7. Apply the style **Heading2** to the subheadings, **Rocks**, **Glaciation** and **Civilisation**.

8. Print a copy of the document.

9. Save the document as **Lakes4** and close it.

Exercise 3.20

1. Open the document **Hall**.

2. Select the whole document and apply the style **Halltext**.

3. Apply the style **Hallhead** to the main title for the document.

4. Apply the style **Hallsub** to the first subtitle in the document (**The House**).

5. Use format painter to apply the **Hallsub** style to all other subtitles in the document.

6. Set the top page margin only to **5cm**.

7. Insert **Page Breaks** before the subheadings **The Gardens** and **Pets' Corner**.

8. Save the document as **Hall2** and close it.

9. Is there any limit to the number of page breaks that can be inserted on a single page?

10. What are the two types of page orientation called?

Mail Merge

These exercises include topics taken from the following list: creating a main document, creating a data source, editing the main document, and performing mail merge.

Exercise 3.21

1. In a new blank document, type the following letter which is to be the main document of a mail merge. Leave spaces in place of each item of bracketed text.

> (Title) (First Name) (Last Name)
> (Address Line 1)
>
> Dear (First Name)
>
> Congratulations (First Name). You have been uniquely selected to receive one of our completely free holidays. Contact us on the number below and wait for your tickets.
>
> Yours sincerely
>
> Dawn Waldram
>
> 791 512116673

2. Save the document as **Offer**.

3. Create a data source file (recipients list) containing the field names **Title**, **First Name**, **Surname** (or **Last Name**) and **Address Line 1**.

4. Add three fictitious names and addresses to the file. Save this data source (recipient list) as **Test** in the supplied data folder.

5. Insert the data source field names in the appropriate positions in the **Offer** document and save the document again.

6. Merge the **Offer** document and the **Test** data source to produce three letters.

7. Print a copy of the three letters.

8. Save the resulting merged file as **Letters3**.

9. Close all files, saving if prompted.

Exercise 3.22

1. Open the document **Interview**. Instead of sending this letter to one person it is to be used in a mail merge operation.

2. Assign the **Interview** document as the main document in a mail merge process.

3. Open the file **Applicants** as the data source (recipients list).

4. Edit the data and delete the record for **Rula Petrovka**.

5. Change the interview time for Tom Clinkard to **11:00**.

6.   Add your own details to the list. Your interview is for the position of **Operator** at **10:00** on **Wednesday 7th September**.

7.   Delete all the data from the **Interview** document which is specific to Ron Springs, and replace it with the relevant merge fields from the data source.

8.   Merge the **Interview** document and the **Applicants** data source to produce four letters.

9.   Print a copy of the four letters.

10.   Save the resulting merged file as **Letters4**.

11.   Close all files <u>without</u> saving.

Objects

These exercises include topics taken from the following list: inserting a picture, inserting an image from file, inserting charts, moving and resizing a picture, image or chart.

Exercise 3.23

1.   Open the document **Ballet**.

2.   Position the cursor on the blank line underneath the title.

3.   Locate and insert the clip art image of a duck as shown here.

4.   If this clip art cannot be located there is a copy in the supplied data files named **duck.gif**. This can be inserted from file instead.

5.   Resize the image to approximately **8cm** by **4cm**.

6.   Cut the picture from its current location and paste it on a new line at the end of the document.

7.   Copy the image and paste the copy alongside the original.

8.   Resize the first image using the handle in the centre of the top edge until it is half the height but the same width.

9.   Resize the copied image using the handle in the centre of the right edge until it is half the width but the same height.

10.   Which handle would be used to resize the image and maintain its proportions?

11.   Save the document as **Ballet3** and close it.

Exercise 3.24

1. Start a new *Word* document.

2. Type the following heading (centred and bold):

    Outdoor Supplies Company

    Sales Performance (thousands)

3. Insert a chart under this heading using the following datasheet.

	Qtr 1	Qtr 2	Qtr 3	Qtr 4
Clothing	25	32	39	44
Equipment	16	26	33	30

4. Increase the size of the chart, maintaining the aspect ratio, until it is approximately **7cm** high.

5. Centre the chart on the page.

6. Insert 3 blank lines after the chart and then insert the image **Outdoor.gif** from the supplied data.

7. Resize the **Outdoor** image to be **4cm** high.

8. Format the **Outdoor** image to have a **Layout** of **Square**.

9. Move the **Outdoor** image into the top right corner of the page.

10. Save the document as **Outdoor** and close it.

Revision Series
© CiA Training Ltd 2005

3

The following revision exercises can involve processes from any part of the ECDL/ICDL Syllabus 4 Module 3: Word Processing.

Exercise 3.25

1. The bar that contains information such as the page and section number of the current page is called what?

    a) Menu Bar

    b) Toolbar

    c) Scroll Bar

    d) Status Bar

2. Start a new *Word* document.

3. Type the following verses. Make the title and each verse a separate paragraph with soft returns at the end of the first three lines of each verse.

    Jack and Jill

    Jack and Jill went up the hill
    To fetch a pail of water;
    Jack fell down and broke his crown,
    And Jill came tumbling after.

    Up Jack got and home did trot,
    As fast as he could caper;
    Went to bed and bound his head,
    With vinegar and brown paper.

4. Make the title **bold**, **centred** and **underlined**.

5. Remove any blank lines from the text and apply formatting so that there is a **12pt** space after each paragraph.

6.   Change the font of the whole document to **Comic Sans MS**.

7.   Insert a relevant clipart picture below the text and resize to a suitable size.

8.   **Centre** the text of the verses and the picture.

9.   Save the document as **Rhyme**.

10. Open the document **Apply**. This is a general job application letter that is going to be sent out to several companies who have been advertising vacancies. The letters are to be produced using a mail merge process.

11. Add your address and the date as right justified lines of text above the first line of the document.

12. Change the font of the whole document to **Arial 12pt**.

13. **Justify** the main text of the letter.

14. Replace the name Emma Jones with your own.

15. Spell check the document and correct any misspellings.

16. Create the following data source:

Contact	Company	Vacancy
Ms Chapman	Metal Products	Shift Manager
Mr Ridley	Ridley Engineering	Team Leader
Mr Rigg	Consolidated Chickens	Supervisor

17. Save the data source as **Vacancies**.

18. Add the fields to the **Apply** document so that the contact, company and vacancy appear in the appropriate places in the letter. Save the letter as **Apply2**.

19. Mail merge the **Apply** document and the **Vacancies** data source.

20. Preview the resultant letters.

21. Print the document.

22. Save the merged document as **Applications**.

23. Close any open documents, saving as necessary.

Exercise 3.26

1. Start *Word*.

2. Open the document **Holiday Plan**.

3. Replace all occurrences of **AnyTown** with **Learnersville**

4. **Underline** and **centre** align the title.

5. Change the font of the whole document to **Arial**, **12pt**.

6. Divide the text into paragraphs after the word **visit** (second sentence) and after the word **beach** (in the list of places).

7. Press <**Enter**> before each of the items in the list of places to visit so that the places become a vertical list.

8. Format the list as a bulleted list.

9. Change the case of the items in the list to **Title Case**.

10. Add a **6pt** space after all paragraphs in the document.

11. Insert the image file **Beach** underneath the text.

12. **Centre** the image and enlarge it so that is **5cm** high.

13. Underneath the image, add a centred underlined title of **Timetable**. Use a key press to make sure this title always appears at the top of a new page.

14. Add the following data into a table underneath the title. Make sure it is **Arial 12pt**.

Day	AM	PM
Mon	Beach	Harbour
Tue	Beach	Shopping
Wed	Art Gallery	Museum
Thurs	County Fair	County Fair
Fri	Harbour	Park
Sat	Beach	Shopping

15. Shade the top row and the left column **Pale Blue**.

16. Underneath the table, add a centred underlined title of **Weather Forecast** in **Arial 12pt**. Make sure this title always appears at the top of a new page.

17. Add the following chart after the new title:

	Mon	Tue	Wed	Thu	Fri	Sat
% chance Sun	70	50	20	50	70	90
% chance Rain	30	50	80	50	30	10

18. Increase the chart width so that all data and labels are fully displayed.

19. Set the page margins to **2.5cm**.

20. Set your name as the document author.

21. In the document footer, add the date to the left and page numbers on the right.

22. Print one copy of the document.

23. Save the document as **Holiday Plan2** and close it.

Exercise 3.27

1. Open the document **Report**. This the draft for a report created by Learnersville council concerning the popularity of existing facilities and suggestions for new ones. It requires some work before it can be submitted.

2. Apply the style **Reporthead** to the title.

3. Apply the style **Reporttext** to the remaining text.

4. Insert a table of 5 columns and 5 rows between the first and second paragraphs of text.

5. Enter the following text into the table.

Facility	Visitors	Enjoyed	Disliked	Neutral
Harbour	560	70%	10%	20%
Beach	850	80%	5%	15%
Art Gallery	436	72%	20%	8%
Park	320	40%	55%	5%

6. Add the following extra row to the table.

County Fair	510	65%	15%	20%

7. Embolden the top row.

8. Shade the top row **dark blue** and change the text colour of the top row to **white**.

9. Insert a chart after the second paragraph of text, based on the following datasheet:

		A	B	C	D	E
		Aquarium	Pier	Zoo	Other	
1	Votes	214	552	130	94	
2						

10. By dragging only the side edge of the final chart, resize it to be almost the full width of the text (about **15cm** wide).

11. Make sure the third paragraph, starting **Also included**, always starts on a new page.

12. Locate the image **Beach** from the supplied data and insert it after the end of this paragraph.

13. Centre the image on the page and resize the picture, making it **8cm** wide.

14. Cut the text for the complete letter at the end of the **Report** document, and paste it into a new blank document.

15. Change the font of the new document to **Arial 12pt black**.

16. Save the document as **Thanks**.

17. The letter is to be merged with the names and addresses in the file **Names**. Include the merge fields **Name**, **Address**, **Town** above the text **Dear Visitor**.

18. Amend the data source to add your own name and address.

19. Merge the document and data source and print the first two merged letters.

20. Save the merged document as **Thanksmerge**, then close it. Don't save the other merge documents.

21. Print one copy of the **Report** document, save it as **Report2** and close it.

Exercise 3.28

1.   Open the document **Science**. This is the first part of a school science project.

2.   Add the title, **Biology Project - Bill Barnacle**

3.   Centre the text.

4.   Underline the title and change the font size to **14**.

5.   Indent the first line of the first paragraph by **1.5cm**.

6.   Replace the word **Biology** with **Science** throughout.

7.   Use the data in the composition table to create a chart directly underneath it.

8.   Increase the <u>width</u> of the chart only, until all the labels on the axes can be seen.

9.   Centre the chart on the page.

10. Insert a page break before the last line of text on the page.

11. Insert a new line after the last line of text and create Left Tabs at **4**cm and **10**cm.

12. Using those tabs, create a tabbed list from the following:

Oxygen	O2
Nitrogen	N2
Argon	Ar
Carbon Dioxide	CO2
Neon	Ne
Methane	CH4
Helium	He
Krypton	Kr
Hydrogen	H2

3

13. Make the list into a bulleted list using any symbol as the bullets.

14. Apply a **3pt Shadow** border around the list.

15. Format the list to have a right indent of **3cm** and a **6pt** after paragraph spacing.

16. For every symbol in the list where a number occurs, e.g. **O2**, format the number as a subscript, e.g. **O_2**.

17. Locate the entries for carbon dioxide and methane and format them as **italic**. The list should now look something like this:

• Oxygen	O_2
• Nitrogen	N_2
• Argon	Ar
• *Carbon Dioxide*	*CO_2*
• Neon	Ne
• Helium	He
• *Methane*	*CH_4*
• Krypton	Kr
• Hydrogen	H_2

18. Select the whole document and change the font to **Arial** and the line spacing to **1.5** lines.

19. Select the first two paragraphs and justify the text.

20. Add page numbers to the right of the document footer.

21. Print a copy of the document.

22. Change the page orientation to **Landscape** and print another copy.

23. Change back to **Portrait** orientation and save the document as **Science2**.

24. Save the document again with the same name but as a Web Page (***.htm** extension). If a message appears about features not being supported, click **Continue**.

25. Close the document.

Exercise 3.29

1. Start a new *Word* document. This is to be a mail merged letter sent out to patients of a health centre, informing them of their appointments and requesting the completion of a questionnaire.

2. Type the following:

LearnersVille Health Centre

LearnersVille

LV4 53F

17 August 2005

Dear

You have successfully reserved the following appointment time   on   . You will be seeing   . Please let us know   hours before the appointment if you have to rearrange the appointment.

Please find enclosed a short questionnaire to help us improve facilities for visitors to the health centre. If you could bring the completed form with you we would be most grateful.

Yours sincerely

LearnersVille Health Centre.

3. Format the letter as **Arial 10pt** and justify the main body of text.

4. Save the document as **Appointment**.

5. Create the following data source as a sample for the merge process:

Title	Initial	Last name	Time	Date	Staff	Hours
Mr	F	Bathurst	11:00am	11/09/05	Dr Chapman	48
Miss	J	Lilly	09:00am	16/10/05	Nurse Rigg	24
Ms	L	Grant	15:00pm	24/10/05	Dr Waldram	48

6. Save the data source as **Patients**.

7. Insert the field headers at the relevant sections.

8. Mail merge the two documents together.

9. Save the merged documents as **Appointment Letters**.

10. Close all open documents <u>without</u> saving.

11. Open the document **Questionnaire**.

12. Underline, embolden and centre the first line.

13. Change the font for the whole document to **Verdana**.

14. Format the first two questions only to have a right indentation of **4cm**. This will leave space for answers to be entered.

15. In the table make the top row bold and the give the left hand column a **pale green** background.

16. Add a **1.5pt** border around all the remaining cells, i.e. the cells where input is possible.

17. On the line with the **Age range** question, add left tab marks at **5cm**, **7.5cm**, **10cm** and **12.5cm** then insert tabs so that the four ranges line up with them.

18. Add a new line under this with the same tab marks, and insert four ⬜ symbols so that they line up under the four ranges. The symbol can be found in the **Wingdings** font, code 113. Change the font size for this line to **20pt**.

19. Open the **News** document.

20. Copy all the text and paste it at the end of the **Questionnaire** document.

21. Copy the existing formatting of the **Questionnaire** document to the new text using the format painter.

22. Copy the Health Centre logo from the **News** document and place it after the end of the text in the **Questionnaire** document.

23. Close the **News** document <u>without</u> saving.

24. In the **Questionnaire** document, delete the **News Flash** title.

25. Make the list of alternative locations into a numbered list.

26. Right align the image.

27. View the document header. Insert the word **Questionnaire** at the left of the header and insert the current date as a field at the right.

28. Print one copy of the document.

29. Save the document as **Questionnaire2** and close it.

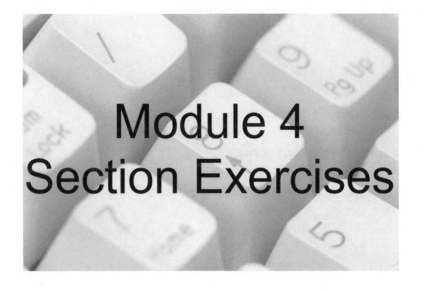

Module 4
Section Exercises

4

The following revision exercises are divided into sections, each targeted at specific elements of the ECDL/ICDL Syllabus 4 Module 4: Spreadsheets. The individual sections are an exact match for the sections in the ECDL/ICDL Syllabus 4 Guides from CiA Training, making the guides an ideal reference source for anyone working through these exercises.

Getting Started

These exercises include topics taken from the following list: starting and closing *Excel*, using menus, toolbars and help, the worksheet window, moving around a worksheet and setting preferences.

Exercise 4.1

1.   Close down *Excel*, if in use.

2.   Start *Excel* using the **Start** button.

3.   Use the mouse pointer to find **ToolTips** for the following buttons:

a)

b)

c)

d)

4.   How many options are listed within the **Format Menu**?

5.   Display the **Forms Toolbar**.

6.   Use the **Help** command to display the help window and find out what an **Add-In** is (Tip: use the **Contents** or the **Index** tab).

7.   Close the **Forms Toolbar**.

8.   Close down *Excel*, what did you do?

Exercise 4.2

1. Start *Excel*, if not open.

2. Use the mouse pointer to find **ToolTips** for the following buttons:

    a)

    b)

    c)

    d)

3. Display the **Picture Toolbar**.

4. With a key press move to the last column of a blank worksheet. What did you press? What is the last column?

5. Move down to the last row, what is the row number?

6. What key press always returns to a cell in column **A**?

7. What key press is used to move one screen to the right?

8. Hide the **Picture Toolbar**.

9. Use **Help** to find out the maximum number of columns in a worksheet (**worksheet size**).

10. How many different ways are there to close down *Excel*?

11. Close down *Excel*.

Open and Close Workbooks

These exercises include topics taken from the following list: opening and closing workbooks, using scroll bars and opening multiple workbooks.

Exercise 4.3

1. Open the workbook **Grand Hotel**. Maximise the window if necessary.

2. Use the scroll bars to navigate to the edges of the main block of occupied cells. What is last cell reference (bottom right corner) in the main block?

3. Navigate to the **Bookings** block to the right. What range of cells does it occupy (excluding the **Bookings** label in cell **Q2**)?

4. What is the current rate of **Tax** for **Jan to Mar**, located in cell **R17**, as a percentage?

5. Make **A1** the active cell in the **Grand Hotel** workbook.

6. Scroll down with the scroll button to display **Row 15** as the first row on the screen. What cell contents are displayed at the top left of the screen?

7. Leave the **Grand Hotel** workbook open and open the workbook **Budget**.

8. What is the total **Net Profit** for the year?

9. Make **Grand Hotel** the active workbook.

10. Close the workbook **Grand Hotel** <u>without</u> saving.

11. Close the workbook **Budget** <u>without</u> saving.

Exercise 4.4

1. Open the workbook **Hydrogen**.

2. Open the workbook **Market Stall**.

3. Both the workbooks are now open. The **Taskbar** along the bottom of the screen shows each open workbook as a button. If these buttons are not displayed on the **Taskbar**, then select **Tools | Options | View** tab and check **Windows in Taskbar**. Click **OK**.

4. Which of the workbooks is active, denoted by the button representing the workbook appearing to be pressed?

5. Click on the **Hydrogen** button to view that workbook. This workbook is now active.

6. Open the workbook **Temperatures**. The **Taskbar** now shows three workbooks as buttons.

7. Which workbook on the **Taskbar** appears to be pressed?

8. Display **Market Stall**.

9. Use the scroll bars to navigate to the edges of the block of occupied cells. Which is the last occupied cell?

10. Use a key press to return to cell **A1**. What did you press?

11. Close all the open workbooks <u>without</u> saving.

Creating and Saving Workbooks

These exercises include topics taken from the following list: starting a new workbook, entering numbers and labels, saving a new workbook, saving a named workbook and saving as a web page.

Exercise 4.5

1. Start with a new workbook.

2. Create the following worksheet in the columns and rows indicated.

	A	B	C	D	E
1	Breakdown of TV Viewing Figures				
2					
3		Channel	Percentage		
4		Channel1	28		
5		Channel2	17		
6		Channel3	45		
7		Channel4	6		
8		Channel5	4		
9					

3. Save the workbook as **Viewing**.

4. Resave the workbook as **Viewing.csv** and close it.

5. Open the generic file **snackdata.csv**.

6. Save the file as a workbook **snackdata.xls**.

7. Close the workbook.

Exercise 4.6

1. Start a new workbook.

2. Create the following worksheet in the columns and rows indicated.

	A	B	C	D
1	CLIMATE	Adelaide, Australia		
2		RAINFALL	TEMP	
3	Months	(cms)	(C)	
4	January	1.8	22	
5	February	1.8	22	
6	March	2.5	22	
7	April	4.0	21	
8	May	7.0	17	
9	June	8.0	12	
10	July	7.0	11	
11	August	6.0	11	
12	September	5.0	13	
13	October	4.5	16	
14	November	3.0	18	
15	December	2.5	21	
16				

3. Save the workbook as **Adelaide**.

4. Re-save the workbook as a **Web Page**, named **Adelaide Weather**.

5. Close the workbook.

6. Preview the web page, **Adelaide Weather** in a browser.

7. Close the browser.

Formulas

These exercises include topics taken from the following list: creating formulas, using brackets, **AutoSum** and checking for errors.

Exercise 4.7

1. On a blank worksheet enter the numbers in the cells to match below.

	A	B	C	D	E
1	**Course Attendances**				
2					
3		Term1	Term 2	Term 3	Total
4	Spanish	20	12	5	
5	Pottery	8	9	7	
6	Yoga	15	18	16	
7	Self Defence	6	11	16	
8	All Courses				
9					

2. Click in cell **B8**. Use a formula to add the four cells above. What is the total?

3. Click in cell **E4**. Click the **AutoSum** button. Press **<Enter>**. What is the answer?

4. Complete cells **C8**, **D8**, **E5**, **E6** and **E7**.

5. Click in cell **E8**. **AutoSum** is to be used to sum the column or the row of totals. Will it sum the column or the row?

6. Click the **AutoSum** button, press **<Enter>**. What is the answer?

7. Delete the contents of **E8**. Use **AutoSum** again but click and drag to select the row of numbers, **B8:D8**. What is the answer? Is it the same answer as before?

8. Save the workbook as **Courses** and then close it.

Exercise 4.8

1. Start a new workbook.

2. Create the following worksheet.

	A	B	C	D	E	F
1	Computer Equipment Sales					
2						
3	Sales	PCs	Printers	Scanners	Modems	Total Units
4	John	9	3	2	3	
5	Natalie	5	5	4	0	
6	Asif	7	2	5	0	
7	Craig	10	1	0	1	
8	Alex	3	7	3	1	
9	Total					
10						

3. Complete row **9** and column **F**, using **AutoSum**.

4. Add the following data to rows **11** and **12**.

10						
11	Profit per Item	50	20	10	5	
12	Total Profit					
13						

5. Complete row **12** using a formula to calculate the profit made from selling each item.

6. Sum the row to find the overall profit from selling all the items. What is the profit?

7. Enter the salespersons' names again in **A15:A19**. In cells **B15:B19**, calculate the profit made by each salesperson. Who made the most profit for the company?

8. Check all the formulas by double clicking on each in turn.

9. Save the completed workbook as **Computer Sales** and then close it.

Workbooks

These exercises include topics taken from the following list: using multiple sheets, switching between sheets, renaming, copying, moving, inserting and deleting sheets.

Exercise 4.9

1. Open the workbook **Forecast**. This workbook compares an estimate of sales for a three month period against the actual sales. The comparison is shown on the chart worksheet.

2. Display the **Chart** worksheet. How would you describe the attempt at estimating the sales figures: a) within 1000 either way - good, b) more than 1000 over - too optimistic, c) more than 1000 under - too pessimistic.

3. Delete the **Chart** sheet.

4. Copy the **Estimate** sheet to a new workbook.

5. Save the workbook as **Copy** and then close it.

6. Insert a new sheet in the **Forecast** workbook ready to add more detailed information.

7. Rename the new sheet **Accounts**.

8. Move the **Accounts** sheet to be the first sheet in the book.

9. Save the workbook as **Forecast2**.

10. Close the workbook.

Exercise 4.10

1. Open the workbook **Divisions**. This is a workbook that contains six worksheets, each representing a division within a company.

2. Rename **Sheet1** as **North**.

3. Rename **Sheet2** as **Midlands**. Rename all the other sheets with the name of the **Division** contained in cell **B9** of each worksheet.

4. Move the **Midlands** sheet to between **South** and **East**.

5. Move the **South West** sheet to between **North** and **South** as shown.

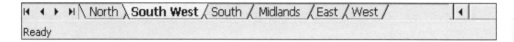

6. Delete the **Midlands** sheet.

7. The company has opened another division. Copy the **South West** worksheet to create a new division.

8. Rename the new worksheet as **South East**.

9. Enter the label **South East** in cell **B9**.

10. Save the workbook as **Divisions2**.

11. Close the workbook.

Revision Exercises

Editing

These exercises include topics taken from the following list: editing and deleting cell content, using undo and redo, using the fill handle, copying and moving cells, finding specific text and replacing text.

Exercise 4.11

1. Open the workbook **Petty Cash**.

2. In cell **E5** enter the formula **=E4-D5** to reduce the **Total** by the amount spent.

3. Copy this formula down the column to cell **E13**.

4. Calculate the difference in cell **E17** between the reducing total and the cash as counted.

5. The difference is not **0**. What is it?

6. After checking the receipts you find that the **Coffee** was **5.50** not **5.00**. Make the change.

7. A receipt was found that had been missed. Add the details **25** of the month, **Office** expense for **Milk** at **12.65**.

8. Copy the formula to **E14** to calculate the **Total**.

9. Adjust the formula in cell **E17**. What is the **Difference** now?

10. The last receipt should be **Miscellaneous**. Copy and paste to make the change.

11. Save the workbook as **Petty Cash Feb**.

12. Close the workbook.

Exercise 4.12

1. Open the workbook **Lists**. This contains a worksheet with three blocks of data: **Names**, **Numbers** and **Alphanumerics**.

2. Leave the original columns as they are, highlight each of the other lists in turn and sort the data according to the labels at the top of each column.

3. Which number comes first in ascending order?

4. Which name comes last in descending order?

5. To compare the three different types of data, copy the three original blocks to form a new continuous column starting in cell **B15**.

6. Sort the new block into ascending order.

7. What type of data comes first?

8. Undo the sort and resort in descending order.

9. With the column still selected, replace all occurrences of **j** with **a**. How many replacements?

10. Re-sort the list in ascending order.

11. Which item is 10th in the list?

12. Experiment with another block of data to determine if upper and lowercase letters have any effect after being sorted.

13. Close the workbook <u>without</u> saving.

4

Printing

These exercises include topics taken from the following list: printing, print preview and page setup, changing margins, adding headers and footers, printing part of a worksheet, adding print titles, setting print options and displaying and printing formulas.

Exercise 4.13

1. Open the workbook **Income**.

2. **Print Preview** the worksheet.

3. Add the filename as a centred header using a code. What is the code?

4. Change the page orientation to **Landscape**.

5. Select to fit to one page.

6. Reduce the left and right margins to **0.5**.

7. Display the formulas.

8. Adjust the columns to display the full contents of every cell.

9. Choose to print the gridlines and the row and column headings.

10. Print a copy of the worksheet.

11. Turn off the formulas, gridlines and row and column headings.

12. Obtain a printout of the first three months only, i.e. range **A1:D16**.

13. Close the workbook <u>without</u> saving.

Exercise 4.14

1. Open the workbook **Grand Hotel**.

2. **Print Preview** the spreadsheet. How many pages are there?

3. Alter the page setup to print the worksheet in **Landscape** and change the side margins to **0.9cm**.

4. Select to print to one page.

5. Cancel the fit option and set the print scaling to **80%**.

6. Remove the footer.

7. The hotel manager is about to start a cost cutting exercise, print out only the details of payments, including the months as titles.

8. The accountant wants to check the formulas for the first six months of the year. Display the formulas, gridlines and row and column headings. Print out the required part.

9. Remove the formulas and switch off the printed gridlines and row and column headings.

10. Print preview the worksheet to check for the normal display.

11. Close the workbook <u>without</u> saving.

4

Formatting

These exercises include topics taken from the following list: adding bold, underline and italic, changing font and font size, formatting numbers and dates, cell alignment, changing row height and column width, inserting and deleting rows and columns, adding borders and colour, rotating cell content, freezing panes and using zoom.

Exercise 4.15

1. Open the workbook **Theatre**. This workbook compares theatre audiences for a specific week for several large cities.

2. Insert a new row **2**.

3. Widen column **A** to display the day labels in full.

4. Adjust columns **B** to **F** to **AutoFit** the data in those columns.

5. Sum the columns and the rows.

6. What was the total attendance for the whole week for all the cities?

7. Which city has the largest attendance for the week?

8. Which day was the most popular?

9. Rotate the text in the range **B3:G3** to **45** degrees.

10. Remove the italic formatting from the range **A4:A9**.

11. Change the height of row **10** to **21.00** units.

12. Change the width of columns **B:G** to **8.00** units.

13. Add dashed borders (**Outline** and **Inside**) and a **light yellow** background to the range **A3:G10**.

14. Change the cell colour of the range **B4:F9** to **light blue**.

15. In cell **A1** increase the font size to **14pt**.

16. Save the workbook as **Theatre2** and close it.

Exercise 4.16

1. Open the workbook **Market Stall**.

2. Change the font size of the title in **A1** to **12pt** and make it **bold**.

3. Freeze column **A**. Scroll to the right to check that column **A** stays on the screen.

4. Format the ranges **B3:N11** and **B13:N14** as currency, no decimal places but include the currency symbol.

5. Format the range **B14:N14** to display negative values in red with a negative sign.

6. Change the width of column **A** to **16.00** units (**117 pixels**).

7. Using zoom, fit the entire worksheet on the screen.

8. Print preview the worksheet. What is the orientation and how many pages are there?

9. Change the setup of the worksheet to display it best on one piece of paper.

10. Save the workbook as **Market Stall Formatted**.

11. Close the workbook.

Functions and Addressing

These exercises include topics taken from the following list: using sum, count, average, maximum, minimum, IF and applying relative, absolute and mixed addressing.

Exercise 4.17

1. Start a new workbook and create the worksheet below.

	A	B	C	D
1	Stationery Sales 1st Quarter			
2				
3		Sold	Price	Sales
4	Pens	456	5.68	
5	A4 Paper	345	3.25	
6	Calculators	23	8.99	
7	Box Files	665	4.99	
8	Pencils	345	0.23	
9	Rulers	89	1.69	
10	Total Sold		Total Sales	
11				

2. **Embolden** the title cells **A1**, **A10** and **C10**.

3. **Right** align and make **bold** the range **B3:D3** and cell **C10**.

4. Complete the **Sales** column by multiplying the number **Sold** by **Price**.

5. Use **AutoSum** to total the **Sales** column.

6. **Centre** the title in cell **A1** across columns **A** to **D**.

7. Increase the font size of the title to **14pt**.

8. In cell **C13** enter the label **Average**.

9.   In cell **D13** calculate the average of the range **D4:D9**.

10. Format cell **D13** to display two decimal places. What is the average value of sales?

11. In cell **C14** enter the label **Highest**.

12. Use a function to display the highest sales.

13. In cell **C15** enter the label **Lowest**.

14. Use a function to display the lowest sales

15. In cell **E3** enter the label **Average +/-**. Widen the column to display all the text.

16. In cell **E4** enter a formula to calculate the difference between the sales and the average in cell **D13**. To be able to copy this formula down the row, edit the formula to fix cell **D13**.

17. Copy the formula down the column.

18. In cell **E10 AutoSum** the column to check that the calculations are correct. The total should be **0**.

19. Save the workbook as **Stationery Sales**.

20. Close the workbook.

Exercise 4.18

1.   Open the **Results** workbook. This worksheet records the percentage scores from tests taken.

2.   Double click in cell **A1** and add your name to the end of the text.

3. In cell **A22** enter the label **Average Mark**.

4. In cell **B22** calculate the average of the marks using a function. What is the average?

5. You were absent for the **Chemistry** test through illness, delete the **0** in cell **B12**. This increases your average as blank cells are not counted. What is the average now?

6. In cell **A23** enter the label **Number of Subjects**.

7. In cell **B23** calculate the number of subjects. The number of subjects is calculated using the **COUNT** function (remember to count the marks, not the subject titles).

8. Add **Highest Mark** in cell **A24** and **Lowest Mark** in cell **A25**.

9. Enter functions in cells **B24** and **B25** to calculate the highest and lowest marks.

10. Enter the label **Pass/Fail** in cell **C3**.

11. Use the **Format Painter** to copy the formats from **B3** to **C3**.

12. The pass rate for each of these examinations is **50** marks. Use the **IF** function in cell **C4** to display **Pass** for marks over **49** and **Fail** for marks **49** and under.

13. Right align the contents of cell **C4**.

14. Copy this formula using the **Fill Handle** down the column to cell **C20**. How many tests resulted in a **Pass**?

15. Print a copy of the worksheet.

16. Save the workbook as **Results2** then close it.

Charts

These exercises include topics taken from the following list: creating charts, embedded charts, changing chart type, formatting and printing charts.

Exercise 4.19

1. Open the workbook **TV**. This contains a breakdown of TV viewing figures.

2. Increase the font size of the text in cell **A1** to **14pt**.

3. Increase the height of rows **3** to **8** to **18.00 units**.

4. Format cell **C3** to wrap the text. Why does cell **C3** not adjust to display all the text?

5. Adjust the height of row **3** to display the label in cell **C3** in full. Right align **C3**.

6. Rename the sheet as **Data**.

7. Highlight the range **B3:C8** and create a **Pie with a 3-D visual effect**.

8. On the **Titles** tab, add the title **TV Viewing Figures**.

9. Remove the **Legend**, but add the **Category name** and **Value** to the **Pie Chart**.

10. Create the **Pie Chart** on the same sheet as the data. Move the chart so that it is under the data.

11. Format the chart title as follows: change the font size to **16pt**, add a **pale yellow background** and add an automatic border.

12. Explode the **Channel2** segment, and then print a copy of the worksheet.

13. Save the workbook as **Chart** and then close it.

Revision Exercises

Exercise 4.20

1. Open the workbook **Temperatures**.

2. Complete row **17**, the average temperatures.

3. Format the range **B17:F17** to display one decimal place.

4. Which city has the highest average temperature and what is it?

5. Chart the temperatures of **London** and **Toronto** as **Clustered Columns**.

6. Add the chart options, Title **Temperatures**, X axis title **Months**, Y axis title **Temps**. Leave the **Legend** displayed on the right.

7. Create the chart on a separate sheet, named **Chart**.

8. Move the **Chart** worksheet to the right of the **Temperatures** worksheet.

9. Remove the colour from the plot area.

10. Change the fill effect of the **Toronto** series to a lined pattern. This helps distinguish the two sets of data when printed in black and white.

11. Print a copy of the chart.

12. How would you describe the two series in relation to each other?

13. Save the workbook as **Temperature Chart** and close it.

Revision Series
© CiA Training Ltd 2005

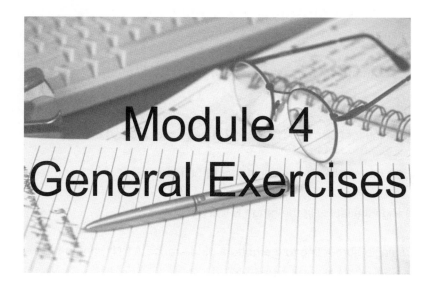

Module 4
General Exercises

The following revision exercises can involve processes from any part of the ECDL/ICDL Syllabus 4 Module 4: Spreadsheets.

Revision Exercises

1. Open the workbook **Cottages**. This workbook contains information about a property company buying, selling and letting holiday cottages.

2. On the **Cashflow** worksheet, widen column **A** to display the data in full.

3. Increase the font size in cell **A1** to **12pt** and make the text bold.

4. Increase the height of rows **1** to **14** to **18.00** units.

5. Right align the labels in the range **B1:M1**.

6. Add a single border line to the bottom of the range **A1:N1**, and a top and bottom line to the ranges, **A4:N4** and **A12:N12**.

7. In late February wind blew the roof off four cottages. The **Repairs and Maintenance** costs were **1,700** for **February** and **5,000** for **March**; make the changes.

8. Use a formula to add together the cells **B2** and **B3** in cell **B4**. Copy the formula in cell **B4** to the range **C4:N4**.

9. Enter a function in cell **B12** to calculate the total for the range **B5:B11**.

10. Copy the function in cell **B12** to the range **C12:N12**.

11. To calculate the **Profit** in cell **B13**, subtract the contents of cell **B12** from the contents of **B4** and then copy the formula to the range **C13:N13**.

12. The cumulative profit for January in cell **B14** is simply a copy of the cell above - enter the formula **=B13**.

13. The February cumulative profit in cell **C14** is the January figure plus February's profit, i.e. **=B14+C13**; enter this formula. Copy this formula in cell **C14** to the range **D14:M14**.

14. The **Total Cumulative Profit** in cell **N14** is the same as for **December** in cell **M14**. Enter the formula.

15. Freeze the titles in column **A** so that the labels are always in view.

16. In cell **M17** add the text **Percentage Profit**. **Right** align the data in the cell.

17. Calculate the **Profit** as a percentage of the **Turnover** (cell **N13** divided by cell **N4**) in cell **N17**.

18. Format the percentage in cell **N17** to one decimal place. What is it?

19. Insert the text **Cashflow for Holiday Cottages** into the header of the **Cottages** worksheet. Change the orientation of the worksheet to landscape and make sure it prints on one page only.

20. Print a copy of the **Cottages** worksheet.

21. Using the **Lettings** worksheet, create a line chart from the range **A3:B15**, placed on the worksheet with the data, with the chart title **Lettings**.

22. Move the chart up and to the right of the data. Resize the embedded chart, until the names of all of the months across the **x** axis are displayed.

23. Save the workbook as **Holiday Cottages** to a floppy disk.

24. Close the workbook.

25. Close *Excel*.

Exercise 4.22

1. Open the workbook **Wines**. This workbook contains information about a small wine shop.

2. Save the workbook as **Wine Warehouse** to a floppy disk.

3. On the **Wines** worksheet, adjust the width of column **A** to display the data fully.

4. Change the font colour of the range **A3:G3** to **blue**.

5. Cell **F3** contains a large label for a column of small numbers; wrap the text in cell **F3**.

6. **Right** align the labels in the range **E3:G3**.

7. Make the contents of cell **A1 bold**.

8. Change the **zoom** to **90%**.

9. In cell **G4**, complete the formula to determine the value of the wine by multiplying cell **E4** by cell **F4** (price x stock level).

10. Copy this formula to the range **G5:G25**.

11. Format the range **G4:G25** to display as currency with the appropriate symbol and two decimal places.

12. The manager has decided to reduce the price of two wines to make them wines of the month. Change the **W05** price to **6.59** and the **R10** to **7.99**.

13. After stock taking, two of the levels were found to be incorrect; adjust the stock levels of **R04** to **80** and **W08** to **59**.

14. Sort the range **A3:G25** by **Name** in ascending order.

15. Calculate the total cost of the wine in stock in cell **G26**, using an appropriate function. Add a cell border of a single top line and double bottom line to cell **G26**.

16. Adjust the height of row **26** to **18** units.

17. On the **Sales** worksheet, correct the error in the formula in cell **F26**.

18. In cell **A28**, enter the label **Highest** and use a function to calculate the highest number in the range **B4:B25** (**Week1**).

19. In cell **A29**, enter the label **Lowest** and use a function to calculate the lowest number in the range **B4:B25**.

20. In cell **A30**, enter the label **Average** and use a function to calculate the average number of the sales in the range **B4:B25**. Format cell **A30** as a number with no decimal places.

21. Copy these three functions across the next **4** columns.

22. What is the best selling wine in the whole four week period?

23. On the **Sales** worksheet move the contents of cell **A1** to **A3**.

24. Delete the unwanted rows **1** and **2**.

25. Highlight the two ranges **A1:A23** and **F1:F23** to create a clustered column chart of the wine sales. Amend the chart title to **Total Sales** and remove the **Legend**. Create the chart as an object on the **Sales** worksheet.

26. Move the chart to the right of the data and resize it to display all of the x axis labels.

27. Remove the **Plot Area** colour.

28. Click away from the chart and change the **Page Setup** to display the worksheet in **Landscape**, with left and right margins as **0.5cm**, a centred header - **Sales Week1 to Week4**, add your name in the left section of the footer and scale the worksheet to fit on one page.

29. Print a single copy of the **Sales** worksheet displaying the data and the chart.

30. Save the current position of the workbook using the same file name **Wine Warehouse** and then close it.

31. Close *Excel*.

Exercise 4.23

1. Open the workbook **Tournament**. This workbook contains information and the results of a Tenpin Bowling competition. The handicap column is a number that is added to each game score to try and level the different abilities.

2. **Centre** align the range **E4:E31**.

3. Change the font in cell **A1** to **Times New Roman** and the font size to **16pt**.

4. Rename **Sheet1** as **Entries**.

5. In cell **D32** use an appropriate function to total all the entry fees.

6. Two people have not turned up for the tournament, delete the rows where the **Registered** column contains **N**.

7. In cell **C32** enter the label **Entries** and in cell **D32** use a function to determine the number of bowlers. How many entries are there?

8. Note the amount of fees collected, display **Sheet3** and enter the amount of fees in cell **C5**.

9. Rename **Sheet3** as **Accounts**.

10. Calculate the total income in cell **C6**, using a simple formula to add the cells.

11. Use an appropriate function in cell **C15** to total the range **C9:C14**.

12. In cell **B19**, enter the text **Prize Fund** and in cell **C19** use a formula to find the difference in total income (cell **C6**) and total expenditure (cell **C15**). What is the value of the prize fund?

13. This fund is to be shared in the following way: half to the winner, a third to the second and a sixth to the third. In cell **C21** enter a formula to divide the prize fund by **2**, in cell **C22** enter a formula to divide the prize fund by **3** and in cell **C23** enter a formula to divide the prize fund by **6**.

14. Note the three values and enter them in the range **C10:C12** (be careful as the calculated values will change reducing to **0** when complete). The total income and total expenditure should now be the same.

15. The calculations are no longer needed. Delete the range **B19:C23**.

16. On the **Accounts** worksheet, create a standard **Pie chart** of the expenditure range, **B9:C14**.

17. Include the chart title **Breakdown of Expenditure** and add percentages as **Data Labels**. What percentage of the expenses is the **First Place** prize money?

18. Display **Sheet2**. Rename the sheet **Results**.

19. Format the labels **K3:L3** to wrap the text.

20. **Right** align the range **D3:L3**.

21. Display the **Entries** sheet and copy the range **A4:C29** to the **Results** sheet, starting in cell **A4**.

22. Widen column **A** to display the names in full.

23. Open the workbook **Bowling Scores**.

24. Copy the range **B5:G30**. Switch back to the **Tournament** workbook and paste the range to the **Results** worksheet, starting in cell **D4**.

25. On the **Results** worksheet in cell **J4** total the six games, i.e. **D4:I4**. Copy this formula to the range **J5:J29**.

26. In cell **K4** enter a formula to calculate the **Total Handicap**, which is the contents of cell **C4** multiplied by **6**. Copy this formula to the range **K5:K29**.

27. Add the **Total** and the **Handicap Total** in cell **L4**. Copy this formula to the range **L5:L29**.

28. The results are now complete; sort the block of data, descending, using column **L** the **Grand Total**. The winners are at the top of the list.

29. Insert a new worksheet. Rename the new worksheet **Roll of Honour**.

30. On this worksheet, list the 1st 2nd and 3rd prize winners with their winnings. Format the list appropriately.

31. Display the **Results** worksheet. There is a prize for the highest score for each game. Use a function at the bottom of each **Game** column to display the highest score.

32. Locate the winning names for each of the six games and transfer them to the **Roll of Honour** worksheet. The prize for each high game is **25**.

33. Save the workbook as **Tournament Results** and close it.

34. Close the **Bowling Scores** workbook.

Exercise 4.24

1. Open the workbook **World Cup**. This includes attendance, a league table and income for a major world sporting event held in Canada.

2. On the **Attendance** worksheet in cell **A9** enter your country, or a different country if yours is in the list.

3. Copy cell **A9** and paste to cell **A6** in the **Table** worksheet.

4. In the **Attendance** worksheet, format the cell **A1** to be **bold**, **blue** font colour, font size **16pt** and the font **Times New Roman**.

5. Add a single border to the bottom of the range of cells, **A6:D6**.

6. Format the range **B6:D6** and be **right** aligned and wrap the text of the labels.

7. In cell **D7**, calculate the stadium **Usage** by dividing the **Average Attendance** in cell **B7** by the **Stadium Capacity** in cell **C7**. Copy the formula to the range **D8:D13**.

8. Format the range **D7:D13** as percentages with one decimal place.

9. Create a **Clustered column chart with a 3-D visual effect** of the **Average Attendances** using the range **A6:B13**.

10. Leave the chart title as **Average Attendance** but remove the **Legend**. Add the chart to the **Attendance** worksheet.

11. Move the chart to below the data, to the left. Resize the chart to display all of the **Team** names.

12. Using **Page Setup**, select to print the worksheet on one sheet of paper. Add your name to the left section of the footer and type today's date (not as a code) in the right section of the footer. Select to print the **Gridlines** and the **Row and column headings**.

13. Print one copy of the **Attendance** worksheet.

14. Display the **Income** worksheet.

15. In cell **C20** use an appropriate function to calculate the total number of **Seats Sold**.

16. In cell **D13** calculate, using a formula, the value of the **Lower Tier Ends** seats by multiplying cell **B13** by cell **C13**. Copy this formula to the range **D14:D19**.

17. Complete the **Total Value** in cell **D20**.

18. In cell **B5** add a formula to copy the value in cell **D20** and divide it by **1000**. Display the result as a number with no decimal places.

19. In cell **B8** total the income for the game.

20. Display the **Table** worksheet. This is a league table of the matches played.

21. Wrap the text in the range **B3:H3**.

22. Adjust the width of the columns **B** to **I** to **9 units**.

23. Place the cursor inside the table and sort it in descending order by points.

24. Move the **Table** worksheet to the left of the **Income** worksheet.

25. Save the workbook as **World Cup2** and close it.

Exercise 4.25

1. Open the workbook **Fish**. This workbook contains information on tropical fish, fish tanks and associated costs.

2. Save the workbook as **Tropical Fish**.

3. On the **Tank** worksheet, in cell **E4** enter the formula that calculates the volume of the first tank in litres. Multiply the length, width and height of the tank and then divide by **1000**.

4. Copy the formula to the range **E5:E17**.

5. Format the range **E4:E17** to display the values as numbers to one decimal place.

6. Having completed some background reading, you have decided to buy a tank that holds at least 40 litres of water. Enter **40** in cell **E19**.

7. Increase the height of row **19** to **16.50** units.

8. In cell **G4** enter a function that compares the amount in **E4** with the required amount in cell **E19** (make **E19** an absolute reference to be able to copy down the column). If the tank is not big enough, display **Too small**, otherwise display **OK** (remember to add the speech marks around the text).

9. Copy this function to the range **E5:E16**.

10. You decide to get a bigger tank to offer you more scope. Change the value in cell **E19** to **50**.

11. The tanks are listed in order of tank length. What is the smallest length of tank that matches the requirement?

12. How many of the **14** tanks are **Too small**?

13. Display the **Costs** worksheet and right align the range **A4:G4**.

14. Using an appropriate function, total the costs for **Tank 1**. What is the cost?

15. Copy this function to the range **G6:G18**.

16. Your budget for a tank is **200**. Which tank is the biggest (length) that you can afford?

17. Check the measurements of your chosen tank on the **Tank** worksheet, then display the **Fish** worksheet. Name the fish that would be unsuitable for your tank.

18. Sort the list into alphabetical order using the fish names.

19. Insert a new worksheet.

20. Rename the worksheet **Shopping List**.

21. Copy the range **A3:E3** from the **Tank** worksheet to starting cell **B3** on the **Shopping List** worksheet.

22. Copy the range of your chosen **Tank** to starting cell **B4** on the **Shopping List** worksheet.

23. Copy the range **A4:G4** from the **Costs** worksheet to the **Shopping List** worksheet starting on cell **B7**.

24. Copy the range of the costs for your chosen **Tank** on the **Costs** worksheet to the **Shopping List** worksheet starting on cell **B8**.

25. Widen any columns as necessary to display all the data.

26. Enter the label **Shopping List** in cell **B1**. Format the cell contents to be **14pt**, **Bold** and font colour **blue**.

27. Merge and centre the label in cell **B1** to the range **B1:H1**.

28. On the **Shopping List** worksheet, create a **Pie** chart of the range **C7:G8**.

29. Add a chart title **Cost of Tropical Fish Tank**, remove the **Legend**, and using the **Data Labels** tab, add the **Category names** and **Percentage** to the labels.

30. Create the chart with the data. Move the chart to start at column **B**, under the data.

31. What **Percentage** of the cost involved is for the actual tank?

32. Click away from the chart and print preview the worksheet.

33. Add a customised footer with your name in the centre section and today's date in the right section.

34. Print a copy of the worksheet.

35. Save the workbook using the same name.

36. Display the **Tank** worksheet and delete the contents of cell **E19**.

37. Save the workbook as a template using the same name to a floppy disk.

38. Close the workbook.

39. Close *Excel*.

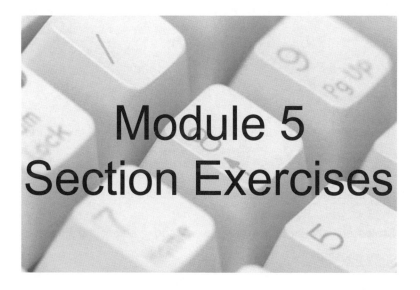

Module 5
Section Exercises

The following revision exercises are divided into sections, each targeted at specific elements of the ECDL/ICDL Syllabus 4 Module 5: Database. The individual sections are an exact match for the sections in the ECDL/ICDL Syllabus 4 Training Guides from CiA Training, making the guides an ideal reference source for anyone working through these exercises.

5

Revision Exercises

Databases

These exercises include topics taken from the following list: starting *Access*, screen layout, **Menus** and **Toolbars**, **Help**, opening databases and tables, closing databases and tables.

Exercise 5.1

1.   Open *Access*.

2.   Open the database **Fixit** from the supplied data files. Make sure the database window is <u>not</u> maximised.

3.   How many tables are in the database and what are their names?

4.   With **Tables** still shown in the database window, select the **File** menu. Which two options are ghosted?

5.   Use the **Help** feature to find information on **Primary Keys**. According to *Microsoft* **Help**, what are the three types of primary key that can be defined?

6.   What is the **ToolTip** shown for the following toolbar button?

7.   Use the **Objects** bar to find how many **Macros** are defined in this database.

8.   What would be the effect of clicking the **Close** button in the very top right corner of the screen?

      a   The database will close but *Access* will stay open.

      b   *Access* will close but the database will stay open.

      c   Both *Access* and the database will close.

9.   Close the database then close *Access*.

Exercise 5.2

1. Open *Access*.

2. Open the database **Central** from the supplied data files.

3. Open the **Premises** table in **Datasheet** view. This shows a list of commercial properties for sale by the Central City Properties Company.

4. How many records are in this table? How can you find this out without counting all the records?

5. How many fields does each record have?

6. What is the address for the record with a **Premises ID** of **P002**?

7. What is the only ghosted option on the **Format** menu?

8. Close the **Premises** table. There should be no prompt to save changes. Which of the following actions would require the table to be saved before closing?

    a   Changing the data in a field.

    b   Adding a new record.

    c   Adding a new field.

    d   Changing a column width.

9. Close the **Central** database.

Tables

These exercises include topics taken from the following list: creating databases and tables, formatting and editing field properties, defining primary keys, creating index fields, entering data, creating validation rules and printing tables.

Exercise 5.3

1. Create a new blank database called **Learning** to be saved in the folder with the supplied data files.

2. Create a new table with the following structure.

Field Name	Data Type	Properties
Course ID	Number	Integer
Description	Text	Length 50
Tutor	Text	Length 20
Basic Cost	Currency	0 decimal places

3. The **Course ID** is always a six character field which contains letters and numbers. Change the data type and properties accordingly. What have you changed?

4. Before saving the table, define **Course ID** as the primary key. What is the main criterion for a suitable primary key field?

5. Save the table as **Courses**.

6. Add another 20 character text field called **Location** to the table design, to appear between the **Tutor** and **Basic Cost** fields.

Revision Series
© CiA Training Ltd 2005

7. Add a validation rule to the **Location** field, so that only entries of **Main**, **Annexe** or **Riverside** will be allowed.

8. Create validation text to list the allowed values if an error is made.

9. Save the table and add the following 3 records. Make sure all data is fully displayed.

Course ID	Description	Tutor	Location	Basic Cost
PH0001	Nuclear Physics	Mr Fletcher	Main	150
PH0003	Astronomy	Ms Starr	Main	100
CH0004	Basic Chemistry	Mr Raman	Annexe	125

10. Close the table and re-open it. Which is the first record in the table? Why?

11. Obtain a print of the table in portrait orientation.

12. Close the table and the database.

Exercise 5.4

1. Create a new blank database called **Hotel** to be saved in the folder with the supplied data files.

2. Use the following data to create a blank table.

Field Name	Data Type	Properties
Guest Name	Text	Length 30
Room No	Number	Integer
Check In	Date/Time	Short Date

3. Save the table as **Register** and let *Access* create a primary key field. What is the name and type of the field *Access* creates?

4. Change the name of the new key field to **Register ID**.

5. Add the following 3 records to the table.

Guest Name	Room No	Check In
Mr Biscuit	21	01/01/2005
Ms Crawley	05	02/06/2005
Mr Banerji	15	02/06/2005

6. Add a new field to the table design as the last field in the table. This field is to hold the number of nights guests will be staying. It is to be called **Nights** and be an **Integer Number** field. Add appropriate data to the table for this extra field.

7. It is decided that the table does not require a primary key. Delete the **Register ID** field. You will need to click **Yes** to all confirmation prompts.

8. Define the **Room No** field as **Indexed** (duplicates allowed).

9. View the table in **Datasheet View**. In what order are the records displayed?

10. Print a copy of the **Register** table showing only the record for Ms Crawley.

11. Close the **Hotel** database.

Table Relationships

These exercises include topics taken from the following list: understanding and applying relationships, creating various types of relationship, deleting relationships, and applying and understanding referential integrity.

Exercise 5.5

1. Open the **Sunshine** database for the Sunshine Apartments Holidays Company. There are two tables: one for apartment records and one for apartment bookings.

2. The tables need to be linked. Examine each table in **Design** view and identify the field that is common to both tables and is suitable to use as a link field.

3. Use this field to create a link between the tables. If the correct field is used, the link will automatically be shown as a **One To Many** relationship in the dialog box.

4. Specify **Referential Integrity** (but no **Cascade** options) for the link.

5. Open the **Apartments** table in **Datasheet** view.

6. Display the subdatasheet for unit **B8**. How many bookings have been taken?

7. Open the **Bookings** table in **Datasheet** view and add a booking for unit **B9** for 7 days from today using your name.

8. What error message prevents this? Which database feature has caused this message?

9. Click **OK** at the message then click **Undo** to cancel the input.

10. Close the table and close the **Sunshine** database.

5

Exercise 5.6

1. Open the **Consultants** database, which holds data for a small IT consultancy company. There are tables for staff records, staff costs, and records of staff expenses against projects.

2. Create a **One To Many** relationship between the **Staff** and **Expenses** tables using **Staff No** field as the linking field.

3. Specify **Referential Integrity** for the relationship.

4. After linking the **Staff** and **Expenses** tables, which one of the following statements is false?

    a   A query can include data from **Staff** and **Expenses** tables.

    b   New **Staff** records cannot be added.

    c   **Expenses** records cannot be added for non-existent staff.

    d   Expenses data is available when viewing **Staff** records.

5. Open the **Staff** table in **Datasheet** view.

6. Display the subdatasheet for employee **112**, **Jason Myers**. How many different projects has Jason included in his expense claims?

7. Create a relationship between the **Staff** and **Cost** tables using **Staff No** field as the linking field.

8. What kind of relationship is created? Why is this?

9. Remove the relationship between the **Staff** and **Cost** tables.

10. Close the **Consultants** database.

Editing

These exercises include topics taken from the following list: moving and changing width of columns, finding text, using wildcards, editing and deleting data, adding and deleting records and using data entry shortcuts.

Exercise 5.7

1. Open the **Beauty** database.

2. Open the **Bookings** table, showing details of bookings taken for a small beauty salon.

3. The data is not fully displayed. Increase the size of all columns as necessary, so that all data can be seen.

4. Move the **Treatment** column so that it appears directly before the **Date** column.

5. Use the **Find** command to find all records with the word **regular** in the **Comment** field. What must the **Match** parameter be set to in order to find the word anywhere within the field? How many records are found?

6. Add new booking record, reference **1413**, for **Joan Branston**. Use a keyboard shortcut to enter all other values exactly the same as the previous record. What key presses are used? Change the **Time** to **15:00**.

7. Anna Li has cancelled her appointment. Delete the record for reference **1407**.

8. Technician **Rose** has left suddenly. Replace her name with **Hortense** in all the relevant records.

9. Close the **Beauty** database.

Exercise 5.8

1. Open the **Club** database.

2. Open the **Membership** table showing details of the club members.

3. Some of the data and column headings are not fully displayed. Widen all necessary columns to rectify this.

4. Move the **Membership Type** and **Discount** fields so that they become the last fields in the table.

5. Change the width of the **Last Name** column to be exactly **20** units. Save the table.

6. Use the **Find** function to find the record for someone living at Orchard Drive.

7. This has been entered in error. Change the address for this record to Apple Drive.

8. **Dawn Jenkins** has been dismissed from the club for inappropriate conduct. Find and delete her record.

9. Add a new record for yourself with the vacant membership number. Use today's date as the **Join Date**, a date next year as the **Next Renewal Date**, **AC** as the **Membership Type**, and no discount.

10. Save the changes to the table and close the **Club** database.

Sorting and Filtering

These exercises include topics taken from the following list: sorting data and using filters.

Exercise 5.9

1. Open the **Consultants** database.

2. Open the **Expenses** table.

3. Sort the table in ascending order of **Cost**. What is the cost for the first (lowest value) record?

4. Sort the table to show the most recent record first. What is the date of the first (most recent) record?

5. Using **Filter By Selection**, display all expenses for the **Metro** project. Print the table showing only these records.

6. Remove the filter. Using **Filter Excluding Selection**, display all expenses that are not **Mileage**. How many records are found?

7. Remove the filter. To highlight large expense claims, filter the table to show expenses of any type for amounts greater than 1000. How many records are found?

8. Remove the filter. Company policy is that no entertaining expenses can be charged against the **Global** project. Filter the table to show only records for the **Global** project that are for **Entertaining**. What is the staff number of the employee who has broken the rules?

9. Remove all filters and sorts and close the **Consultants** database.

Exercise 5.10

1. Open the **Central** database.

2. Open the **Premises** table and make sure all data and labels are fully displayed.

3. Filter the table to show all premises that are not in **Central Area**. How many records are there?

4. Filter the table to show only premises in the **Riverside Complex**.

5. Sort the filtered list in ascending order of **Price**. What is the address of the cheapest property in the **Riverside Complex**?

6. Similarly, show all the **Office Premises**, regardless of location, in descending order of **Unit Area**. How many records are there and what is the **Premises ID** of the largest one?

7. Remove all filters and sorts.

8. Click the **Apply Filter** button. What happens to the data?

9. Remove the filter. Use a filter to find how many unoccupied properties are priced over 100,000.

10. Remove all filters and sorts and close the **Central** database.

Queries

These exercises include topics taken from the following list: create, edit and delete a query, use sort in a query, print query results, query related tables, use value ranges, find non-matches and use AND and OR criteria.

Exercise 5.11

1. Open the **Expenses** database. This has details of expense claims for several IT consultants working on a variety of projects.

2. Create a query based on the **Staff** table to show the fields **Staff No**, **Surname**, **Department**, and **Extension**, in that order. Save the query as **Telephone List** and run it.

3. Edit the **Telephone List** query so that the records are shown in alphabetical order of **Surname**, and the **First Name** field is included between **Surname** and **Department**.

4. Print out the results of the **Telephone List** query in portrait orientation.

5. Create a query based on the **Claims** table to show all the fields for **Miscellaneous** type claims. Save the query as **Check** and run it.

6. Edit the **Check** query so that only miscellaneous claims with a value of greater than 100 are listed.

7. Print out the results of the **Check** query in portrait orientation.

8. The **Check** query may be controversial. Delete it from the database.

9. Create a query based on both the **Staff** and **Claims** tables. Show the fields **Surname**, **Department** from **Staff**, and **Project Code**, **Expense Type** and **Amount** from **Claims**. Sort the results by **Project Code** and save the query as **Detail**.

10. Print out the results of the **Detail** query in **Landscape** orientation.

11. Close the **Expenses** database.

Exercise 5.12

1. Open the **Central** database.

2. Create a query based on the **Premises** table to show the fields **Premises ID**, **Location**, **Address**, **Type of Premises** and **Price**, in that order. Select only **Store Unit** premises in the **Valley Grove** location. Save the query as **Narrow** and run it.

3. Remove all selection criteria, then select all premises with a **Price** between **100,000** and **200,000**. Save the query as **Mid Range** and run it.

4. Edit the **Mid Range** query.

5. Remove all selection criteria then select all **Premises** that are not **Store Units**. Save the query as **Non Store** and run it.

6. Edit the **Non Store** query.

7. Remove all selection criteria then add the field **Floors** to the query grid.

8. Select all **Office Premises** with more than a single floor. Save the query as **Floors** and run it.

9. Print a copy of the **Floors** data then delete the query.

10. Close the **Expenses** database.

Forms

These exercises include topics taken from the following list: Use **AutoForm**, design and create a form, format a form, edit and delete a form, edit data using a form and print from a form.

Exercise 5.13

1. Open the **Club** database.

2. Create a **Columnar AutoForm** based on the **Membership** table. Save the table as **Members1**.

3. Use the **Wizard** to create a columnar form including all the fields from the **Membership** table. Select a **Standard** style and save the form as **Members2**.

4. Use the **New** button in the **Forms** window to create a third form in **Design View**. Include all fields from the **Membership** table in one drag operation to ensure that they are all aligned. Save the form as **Members3**.

5. View each form. The **AutoForm**, **Members1**, may have a different background style as it always uses the last style that was applied to a form. What difference identifies **Members2** and **Members3**?

    Note: The example database in the solutions folder assumes that exercise 5.8 has also been completed. If not, the sequence of fields will be different.

6. Use the **Members2** form to find the record for member **FT167**, Mr Laurence Lamb.

7. Print a copy of the form for this record only.

8. Use the form to delete the record for member **FT167**.

9.   Use the **Members2** form to add a new record to the table, based on the following data:

> **Membership Number FT171, Ms Suzi Li, 2 Chester Buildings. Joined on 15/07/2004, next renewal date 01/08/2005. Membership type AM with 20% discount**.

10. Delete the **Members1** form.

11. Close the **Club** database.

Exercise 5.14

1.   Open the **Central** database.

2.   Use the wizard to produce a columnar form based on all the fields from the **Premises** table. Select the **Standard** style and save the table as **Properties**.

3.   Add a label in the **Form Header** area with the text **Properties Form**.

4.   Format the header label as **Arial**, **18pt**, **Bold**.

5.   Delete the fields **Offices** and **Glazing** from the form.

6.   Click and drag the fields **Floors**, **Lift** and **Parking Places** to the right of the form, underneath the **Comments** field.

7.   Move and resize any fields so that all data and labels are fully displayed.

8.   Reduce the height of the **Detail Area** until it is just large enough to include the remaining fields.

9.   Print the first page of forms. How many records are shown?

10. Close the **Central** database.

Reports

These exercises include topics taken from the following list: Use **AutoReport**, modify and delete a report, preview and print a report, sort data in a report, group data in a report and perform calculations in a report.

Exercise 5.15

1. Open the **Expenses** database.

2. Create a **Columnar AutoReport** based on the **Project** table. Save the report as **Project1**.

3. Edit the **Project1** report and change the **Report Header** label to **Project List**.

4. What fields are shown by default in the **Page Footer** area?

5. Add your name as a label so that it will appear once, on the left underneath the last record on the report.

6. Use the wizard to create a **Tabular** report based on all fields from the **Staff** table. The records are to be sorted first by **Department**, then by **Surname**, with no grouping. Specify **Landscape** orientation and **Corporate** style. Save the report as **Staff1**.

7. Edit the **Staff1** report. Change the **Report Header** to **Department Listing** and remove the **Italic** effect.

8. Delete the **Extension** field from the **Detail** area and its label from the **Page Header**.

9. Print the entire report.

10. Save the report and close the **Expenses** database.

5

Exercise 5.16

1. Open the **Central** database.

2. Use the wizard to create a report based on the **Premises** table using the following criteria:

3. Include only the fields **Premises ID**, **Location**, **Address**, **Type of Premises**, **Occupied** and **Price**.

4. Records in the report are to be grouped by **Location** and sorted by **Price**.

5. Specify that **Price** is to be summed as a **Summary** calculation.

6. Specify **Stepped** layout, **Landscape** orientation and **Corporate** style. Save the report as **Location**.

7. What is the cheapest property in **DockLand**?

8. Use the wizard to produce a similar report, but grouped by **Type of Premises** and saved as **Type**. All other criteria will be the same as for the **Location** report.

9. Would you expect the Grand Total for each report to be the same or different? Why?

10. Edit the **Location** report and change the label in the **Report Header** to **Location Analysis**.

11. Swap the **Location Analysis** label with the date (**=Now()**), so that the date is in the **Report Header** area and the label is in the **Page Footer** area. Change the font size of the date field to **18pt** and make sure it is fully displayed.

12. Print the **Type** report and then delete it.

13. Close the **Central** database.

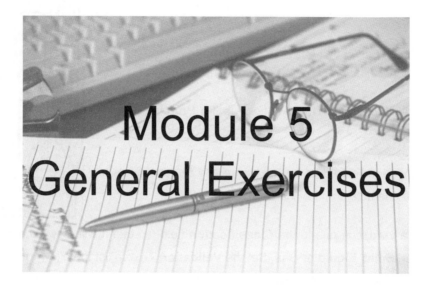

Module 5
General Exercises

The following revision exercises can involve processes from any part of the ECDL/ICDL Syllabus 4 Module 5: Database.

Exercise 5.17

1. Open the database **Chemistry** and open the **Elements** table.

2. One of the columns is not wide enough to display the full heading. Widen the appropriate column.

3. Define the **Atomic Number** field as the **Primary Key** for the table.

4. Change the **Field Size** for the **Name** and **Symbol** fields to be **20** characters and **2** characters respectively.

5. Add a validation rule to the **Classification** field, so that it will only accept entries of **Metal**, **Solid**, **Liquid** or **Gas**. Set the **Validation Text** to list the allowed values in the event of an invalid entry being made.

6. Filter the table to show only **Metal** elements.

7. Sort the filtered data in ascending order of **Melting Point**.

8. Print a copy of the filtered table in portrait orientation then remove all filters/sorts.

9. Add a new record to the table for **Krypton**, with the values shown below:

Atomic Number	Name	Symbol	Atomic Mass	Melting Point	Boiling Point	Classification
36	Krypton	Kr	84	-157	-153	Gas

10. Create a query to show all fields from those elements classified as gases, sorted in alphabetical order of element name. Save the query as **Gases**.

11. Print a copy of the **Gases** query in **Landscape** orientation.

12. Create a query to show **Atomic Number**, **Name**, **Symbol** and **Melting Point** for all elements which melt between **0** and **100** degrees Celsius. Save the query as **Melt**.

13. Create a new table with three fields:

    Atomic Number, **Long Integer Number** field

    Year Discovered, **Long Integer Number** field

    Discovered by, **40** character **Text** field

14. Save the table as **History** and make **Atomic Number** the primary key.

15. Add the following three records to the **History** table:

Atomic Number	Year Discovered	Discovered by
7	1772	Rutherford
12	1755	Davy
32	1886	Winkler

16. Create a relationship between the **Elements** table and the **History** table based on the **Atomic Number** field. What type of link is created?

17. Use the wizard to create a columnar form including all the fields from the **Elements** table. Use any style. Save the form as **Element Data**.

18. Edit **Element Data** and add a title of **Element Data Form** to the **Form Header** area. Include your name at the left edge of the **Form Footer** and save the form.

19. Use the **Element Data** form to find the record for **Sulphur**. Print a copy of the form for the **Sulphur** record only.

20. Use the wizard to create a landscape tabular report showing all the fields from the **Elements** table, grouped by **Classification**. Use any style. Save the report as **List**.

21. Close the **Chemistry** database.

5

Exercise 5.18

1.   Open the database **Hire** and open the **Vehicles** table in datasheet view, showing details of some of the available vehicles owned by a small car hire company.

2.   Make sure all data and headings are displayed in full.

3.   Add a validation rule to the **Type** field so that it will only accept entries of **Compact**, **Family** or **Sports**. Set the **Validation Text** to list the allowed values in the event of an invalid entry being made.

4.   Add a new field to the end of the **Vehicles** table called **Charge**. The data type is to be **Currency** with **0** decimal places.

5.   Add **Charge** data to all existing records according to the following table:

Type	Charge
Compact	50
Family	75
Sports	90

6.   Create a new table called **Bookings** with no primary key, to hold details of vehicle bookings as follows:

Field Name	Data Type	Format
Name	Text	30 characters
Vehicle Number	Number	Long Integer
Start Date	Date	Short Date
Number of Days	Number	Integer

7. Create a relationship between the new **Bookings** table and the **Vehicles** table based on the only field that is common to both tables.

8. Apply referential integrity to the relationship.

9. Use the wizard to create a columnar form including all the fields from the **Bookings** table. Use any style. Save the form as **Booking Form**.

10. Edit the **Booking Form** so that a title of **Booking Entry** appears in the **Form Header** area. Save the form.

11. Use the form to enter the following bookings for vehicles 211, 212, 214 and 313.

Name	Vehicle Number	Start Date	Number of Days
G. Khan	211	29/05/06	3
A. Smith	212	29/05/06	4
D. McKenna	214	02/06/06	5
J. Kirk	313	03/06/06	7

12. Create and run a query which lists all **Compact** vehicles from the **Vehicles** table. Show all fields from the table. Save the query as **Compact**.

13. Print a copy of the result of the **Compact** query.

5

14. Create a query with fields **Vehicle Number**, **Start Date** and **Number of Days** from the **Bookings** table, together with **Type** and **Charge** from the **Vehicles** table. Save the query as **Enquiry**.

15. Print a copy of the **Enquiry** query in **Landscape** orientation.

16. Delete the **Compact** query.

17. Create a **Landscape** orientation report based on all the fields from the **Vehicles** table grouped by **Type** of vehicle and sorted by **Vehicle Number**. Save the report as **Types** and print a copy.

18. Edit the **Types** report. Change the report header to **Vehicle Listing** and remove the **Seats** field (and its heading) from the report.

19. Create a **Landscape** orientation report based on all the fields from the **Enquiry** query. Using the default grouping options, group the report by **Start Date**. Show the sum of **Number of Days** as a summary total. Save the report as **Booking List**.

20. Edit the report so that in the **Page Footer** area, the date appears on the left and your name appears on the right. Remove any other content from the area.

21. Create a calculated field at the right of each report detail line which multiplies the **Number of Days** by **Charge**. Format the field as **Currency**.

22. Save the report and print a copy then close the **Hire** database.

Exercise 5.19

1. Open the database **Wages** and open the **Staff** table.

2. In what sequence are the **Staff** records shown by default? Why?

3. Change the position of the **Department** field in the structure so that it becomes the second field in the table, immediately after the **Staff No** field.

4. Create an index called **Name** based on the **Surname** field in ascending order (this is for practice only and will not reorder the data).

5. Filter the table to show only employees in the **Production** department.

6. Sort the filtered table in ascending order of **Age**.

7. Print a copy of the sorted filtered table then remove all filters/sorts.

8. Filter the table to show only employees who are not in the **Production** department.

9. Sort the filtered table in descending order of **Rate**.

10. Print a copy of the sorted filtered table then remove all filters/sorts.

11. Create a query showing all fields from the **Staff** table, for all employees who have started the company since **1st January 2000**. Save the query as **New Starters** and print a copy of the results.

12. Create a query to see if there are any employees in the **Testing** department who are over **50** years old. Show all fields from the **Staff** table in the resulting list. Save the query as **Old Testers** and print a copy of the results.

13. Create the following table to hold details of the hours worked by each employee.

Field Name	Data Type	Format
Staff No	Number	Long Integer
Date	Date	Short Date
Hours Worked	Number	Integer

14. Save the table as **Hours**, with no primary key.

15. Create a relationship between the **Hours** table and the **Staff** table, based on an appropriate field from each table.

16. Create a report in landscape, on the **Staff** table which has the following format. The report is grouped by **Department**, sorted on **Staff No** and the style is **Compact**. Save the report as **Staff List**.

17. The **Staff List** report will need to be edited so that the title **Department Listing** is shown in the report header.

Department Listing

Department	Staff No	Surname	First Name	Start Date	Age	Rate
Despatch						
	3	Patel	Nora	05.05/1995	48	£18.60
	15	Durralu	Mara	21.09/1995	53	£19.60
	17	Peters	Shaun	31/12/1999	32	£18.60
Finishing						
	6	Kumar	Ravi	27/11/2003	18	£19.60
	9	Singh	Gita	13.01/2000	36	£19.60
	11	Hussan	Tariq	27.09/1995	47	£19.60
	16	Neville	David	13.07/1999	29	£17.50
Maintenance						
	1	Thompson	James	30/12/2002	30	£22.00
	7	Ripley	Ellen	12.06/1998	35	£24.00
	12	Smith	David	18.02/1990	52	£22.40
Production						
	2	Ingam	Ian	24.02/1990	53	£23.20
	4	Tresori	Gina	10.04/2002	37	£20.40
	5	Branson	Paul	01.03/1997	36	£20.40
	8	Jones	Timothy	17/10.2001	43	£20.40
	13	Yomani	Asif	08.05/1999	40	£24.00
	14	Brown	John	08.05/1994	40	£22.40

16 August 2005   Page 1 of 2

18. Paul Branson has left the company. Locate his record in the table and delete it.

19. Add your own details with Paul Branson's old **Staff No**. Assign yourself to the **Production** department with an hourly rate of **20**.

20. Print a copy of the **Staff List** report with your name included.

21. Close the **Wages** database.

Exercise 5.20

1. Open the database **Production**. This database for a small manufacturing company includes a table of the manufacturing output of their three main products for each month of the year and a table to hold orders for their products.

2. Open the **Relationships** window. The link between the **Orders** table and the **Output2005** table is meaningless. Delete it.

3. Change the data type of the **Product** field in the **Orders** table to **Text**, with a length of **20** characters.

4. Create a new relationship between the **Product** fields in the **Orders** and the **Products** tables.

5. Specify **Referential Integrity** for the relationship.

6. Open the **Output2005** table in datasheet view and sort the table by **Month**. Why are the records not in date order? Remove all filters and sorts.

7. Add a new field as the first field in the **Output2005** table. The field name is **Month No**, data type is **Numeric**, **Integer**.

8. Enter appropriate values in the new field for all records, i.e. 1 for January, 2 for February, 12 for December.

9. Sort the amended table by **Month No**.

10. Filter the table to show only sales quantities for the month of **November**.

11. Print the filtered list then remove all filters and sorts.

12. Create a query based on the **Output2005** table showing only sales of **Widgets**, arranged in ascending order of **Quantity**. Show all fields from the table and save the query as **Performance**.

13. Print a single copy of the resulting list.

14. The highest output quantities seem to be in the last 3 months of the year. To see if there are any exceptions, amend the **Performance** query to show records for any product with output greater than **4000** for months before **October**, i.e. month numbers less than **10**. Which records are found? Save the amended query as **Exceptions**.

15. Create a report showing all fields from the **Output2005** table, grouped by **Month No**, sorted by **Product**, showing **Sum** summary values for **Quantity**. The report is to be in **Portrait** orientation, **Formal** style and have a title of **Output by Month**.

16. Amend the report by changing the font of the report title to **Arial**, extending the size of the label if necessary to ensure that the title is still fully displayed.

17. Include your name so that it appears once at the end of the report.

18. Print a copy of the report. Which month has the highest overall total output? What is the overall output quantity for all products for the year?

19. Create another report, similar to **Output by Month**, but grouped by **Product** and sorted by **Month No**. Both **Sum** and **Average** summary values for quantity are to be displayed and the report is to be given a title of **Output by Product**.

20. Amend the report by changing the font of the title to **Arial**, **Italic**. Change the sum and average summary values (and their labels) to **Arial** and their colour to **Red**. Ensure that all data and text is fully displayed. Save the report.

21. Create a simple form which will allow all fields on the **Orders** table to be entered. Save the form as **Order Entry**.

22. Enter an order from **Global Engines Company** for **100 Widgets** with today's date.

23. Print a copy of this order, then close any open objects and close the **Production** database.

Exercise 5.21

1. Open the database **Geography** and open the **Mountains** table in datasheet view, showing details of some of the highest mountains in various parts of the world.

5

2. Make sure that all data and labels are fully displayed.

3. Sort the table in order of date first climbed, with the most recently climbed appearing first in the list. Which was the last of these mountains to be climbed in the nineteenth century?

4. Print a copy of the sorted table.

5. Sort the table in descending order of height and apply a filter so that only mountains higher than **8000** metres are shown. What do they all have in common?

6. Remove all filters and sorts.

7. Create a query which lists all the mountains in the **Alps** range. Show all fields from the table and save the query as **Alps**.

8. Amend the query so that the records are sorted in order of **Height (metres)** and remove the **Height (feet)** field from the output. Save the query.

9. Create another query which shows all mountains between 5000 and 7000 metres high. How many are shown?

10. Save the query as **Medium**.

11. Use the wizard to create a columnar form showing all the fields from the **Alps** query. Select a style of **Expedition** and save the form as **Alpine**.

12. How many records can be viewed using this form?

13. Use the form to find and display the record for the **Matterhorn**. Obtain a print out of the form for this record only.

14. Create the following table to hold details of some of the world's longest rivers.

Field Name	Data Type	Format
Name	Text	Length 50
Continent	Text	Length 50
Starts	Text	Length 50
Ends	Text	Length 50
Length (km)	Number	Long Integer

15. Define **Name** as the primary key and save the table as **Rivers**.

16. Add a record for the river **Nile** in **Africa**, which starts in **Lake Victoria**, ends in the **Mediterranean Sea**, and is **6690km** long.

17. Move the **Length** field in the **Rivers** table so that it appears just after **Continent**.

18. Where necessary, resize column widths so that all data is fully displayed.

19. Change the format of the **Length** field to **Integer**. Save the table.

20. Create a report showing all fields from the **Mountains** table except **Height(feet)** and **First Ascent**, grouped by **Continent**, sorted by **Name**, showing the maximum and minimum mountain height in metres for each continent. The report is to be in **Portrait** orientation, **Formal** style and have a title of **Continents**.

21. Amend the **Continents** report in **Design View** so that it looks similar to the following example. The report title is **24pt** and **red**. The continent names are **14pt bold** and **italic**. A text label has been removed from the continent footer, and some fields and labels have been moved, resized or amended.

5

Peaks of the World

Continent	Name	Country	Range	Height (m)	First Ascent
Africa					
	Kenya	Kenya	Volcano	5199	1899
	Kilimanjaro	Tanzania	Volcano	5895	1889
	Toubkal	Morocco	Atlas	4165	1923
			Min	4165	
			Max	5895	

22. Include your name so that it appears once at the bottom of every page, in the centre of the page.

23. Print a copy of the report.

24. Delete the **Test** query from the database.

25. Close the **Geography** database.

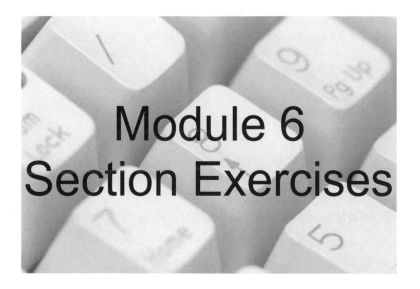

Module 6
Section Exercises

The following revision exercises are divided into sections, each targeted at specific elements of the ECDL/ICDL Syllabus 4 Module 6: Presentation. The individual sections are an exact match for the sections in the ECDL/ICDL Syllabus 4 Training Guides from CiA Training, making the guides an ideal reference source for anyone working through these exercises.

6

Getting Started

These exercises include topics taken from the following list: understanding *PowerPoint* principles, starting *PowerPoint*, using the **AutoContent wizard**, recognising the screen layout, understanding the menus and toolbars, using help, changing preferences and exiting *PowerPoint*.

Exercise 6.1

1. Start *PowerPoint*.

2. What is the name of the area at the top of the screen with labels, e.g. **File**, **Edit**, etc?

3. Use the **What's This?** Help pointer from the **Help** menu to display the help window for the following menu commands and buttons:

    a)   **File | Print**

    b)   **Window | Arrange All**

    c)   **Tools | Options**

    d)   **Format | Font**

    e)

    f)

    g)

4. Use **ToolTips** to discover name of the following buttons:

   a)

   b)

   c)

   d)

5. Use **Help** to find information about **Timings**. How are manual timings set?

6. Close **Help**.

7. Close *PowerPoint*.

Exercise 6.2

1. Open *PowerPoint*.

2. Use the **AutoContent Wizard** to create a **Generic Presentation** with the **Title** of **My First Presentation** and your name in the **Footer**.

3. Name a button on the **Drawing** toolbar.

4. Name a button on the **Picture** toolbar.

5. What does the button do, on the **Picture** toolbar?

6. Ensure the default save location is **My Documents**.

7. Close *PowerPoint*, clicking **No** if prompted to save.

Slides & Presentations

These exercises include topics taken from the following list: understanding and using different views, understanding slide show basics, saving, closing and opening presentations, using presentation/design templates, creating a blank presentation, adding new slides, inserting slides and changing slide layout and background.

Exercise 6.3

1. Open the **Computers** presentation.

2. Switch to **Outline View**.

3. **Collapse All** slides so only the title can be seen.

4. Move the **Printer and Scanner** slide above the **Mouse, Keyboard and Speakers** slide.

5. Switch to **Slide Sorter View**.

6. Move the **Printer and Scanner** slide back to the end of the presentation.

7. Switch to **Notes Page View** and read the notes on each of the pages.

8. Add a **light blue** background to the **Title Slide** of the presentation.

9. Save the presentation as **Computers2** and close it.

Exercise 6.4

1. Create a new blank presentation, selecting the **Title Slide** layout.

2. On the title slide, add the title text **Solar System**.

3. Click to add the **Subtitle 'by Your Name'**.

4. Insert a **New Slide** using the **Title and Text** (**Bulleted List**) layout.

5. Click to add the title **The Sun**.

6. Add a new slide for each of the following titles:

    *   **Mercury**
    *   **Venus**
    *   **Earth**
    *   **Mars**
    *   **Jupiter**
    *   **Saturn**
    *   **Uranus**
    *   **Neptune**
    *   **Pluto**

7. Save the presentation as **Planets**.

8. Close the presentation.

6

Revision Exercises

Formatting

These exercises include topics taken from the following list: applying formatting, text effects and bullets, using undo and redo, changing alignment and spacing, using cut, copy and paste, using animation schemes and custom animation, applying headers & footers, working with master pages and checking spelling.

Exercise 6.5

1. Open the **Computers** presentation.

2. Add a **White Marble Texture Background** to the **Slide Master**.

3. Add a **light blue** background to the **Title Master**.

4. Change the font on the **Slide Master** and **Title Master**.

5. Change the colour of the text of the **Masters** so the text stands out clearly.

6. On the **2nd Slide** add **Custom Animation** to the 2 pictures, so they run as soon as the slide is opened.

7. Add **Custom Animation** to the images on the other slides.

8. Add a **Date** to the presentation which **Automatically Updates** and the **Slide Number** to each slide.

9. Save the presentation as **Computer Formatted** and close it.

Exercise 6.6

1. Open the **Power Shower** presentation.

2. Apply the **Textured Design Template** to the presentation.

3. Copy **Slide 2** and paste it.

4. Add the **Oak Texture** to the background of the new slide **3**.

5. Draw a rectangle which covers all of the text.

6. Change the background colour of the rectangle to **white**.

7. Send the rectangle to the back so the text can be seen.

8. Change the colour of the text to make sure it can be seen clearly against the background.

9. On this slide, **Customize** the **Bullets** to be a **Pen Symbol**.

10. Change the font, colour and size of the title to make it stand out.

11. Change the **Line Spacing** of this slide to be **1.5**.

12. **Centre** the bulleted text.

13. Add your name to the **Footer** of each slide.

14. Check the spelling on the whole presentation.

15. Save the presentation as **Shower Formatted** and close it.

PowerPoint Objects

These exercises include topics taken from the following list: inserting and modifying an organisation chart, moving, resizing and copying objects, inserting and animating **Clip Art**, inserting a picture/chart, using drawing tools and **AutoShapes** on slides, selecting, rotating and flipping objects, arranging and distributing objects, changing object colours and importing images.

Exercise 6.7

1. Open a new blank presentation.

2. Insert an animated **Clip Art**, searching for **Ball**, into the top right of the **Slide Master**.

3. Increase the size of the image and send it to the **Back**.

4. Add an automatically updating date to the bottom of the **Master Slide**.

5. Apply a **Moderate Animation Scheme** to the **Master Slide**.

6. Add 2 more **Ball Clip Art** images to the bottom left of the slide.

7. Reduce the size of the images.

8. Overlap the images and change which one appears on top.

9. Change the colour of the **Title** to **dark red**.

10. Add a **dark red** rectangle around the pictures at the bottom left of the slide.

11. Send this rectangle to the back.

12. Save the presentation as **Images** and close it.

Exercise 6.8

1. Open the **Power Shower** presentation.

2. Move to slide 3, delete the grey text and alter the slide layout to include an organisation chart.

3. Add a chart with the following staff positions:

    Manager with **Assistant Manager**, **Product Manager**, **Sales Manager** and **Customer Services Manager** all as subordinates of the manager.

4. Change the **Organization Chart Style** to **Gradient**.

5. Insert a new, **Title Only** slide at the end of the presentation.

6. Add the title **Office Layout**.

7. Draw a large rectangle below the title to represent the office floor.

8. Select **AutoShapes** | **More AutoShapes** to display room layout shapes.

9. Create an office layout according to the following instructions; moving, rotating and resizing of objects will be required.

10. Place a large, rectangular **Desk** in the centre of the room.

11. Place 8 **Desk Chairs** around the desk, with half of each chair hidden under the desk.

12. Add a **Door Swing** to the bottom left and top right of the room.

13. Add 2 **File Cabinets** to the left wall and a **Floor Lamp** to the bottom right corner.

14. Add a long narrow **Desk** to the top wall.

15. Place a **Telephone** on the long desk.

16. Insert a **Water Clip Art** picture to the first slide.

17. Save the presentation as **Shower2**.

18. Close the presentation.

Slide Shows

These exercises include topics taken from the following list: selecting the correct output format, setting up a slide show, applying slide transitions and timings, running the presentation and printing slides, presentations and handouts.

Exercise 6.9

1.   Open the **Computers** presentation.

2.   Add a suitable **Design Template** to all of the slides.

3.   Add **Random Slide Transitions** to the slides.

4.   View the slide show.

5.   Hide the **Mouse, Keyboard and Speakers** slide.

6.   View the slide show again and during the show, right click and select the hidden slide.

7.   Print all **4** slides on 2 sheets, including their **Notes** pages.

8.   Save the presentation as **Computers3**.

9.   Close the presentation.

6

Exercise 6.10

1. Open the **Tropical Fish** presentation.

2. Change the **Orientation** of the **Slides** to **Portrait**.

3. Apply the **Ocean Design Template** to all of the slides.

4. Apply timings to the slide show.

5. Set up the slide show to **Loop Continuously** and ensure the **Timings** are used.

6. View the slide show to check the timings

7. Apply a different slide transition to each of the pages.

8. View the slide show to view the transitions.

9. Print the slides as handouts with 3 on a sheet.

10. Save the presentation as **Ocean Fish**.

11. Close the presentation.

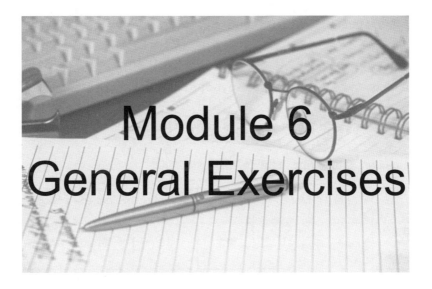

The following revision exercises can involve processes from any part of the ECDL/ICDL Syllabus 4 Module 6: Presentation.

6

Exercise 6.11

1. Open the **Computers** presentation.

2. Move the **Mouse, Keyboard and Speakers** slide to be the final slide of the presentation.

3. Add a further note to the **Mouse, Keyboard and Speakers** slide.

4. Add a new **Title and Chart** slide at the end of the presentation.

5. Edit the chart data to match the following:

	Tower	Monitor	Printer	Scanner	Speakers	Keyboard	Mouse
% of Total Price	52	16	12	10	4	3	3

6. Change the chart to be a **Pie Chart**.

7. Add a background picture, **Leads.jpg** to the **Slide Master**.

8. Add a **light blue** background to the **Title Master**.

9. Insert the **Keyboard.gif** picture at the top left of the **Slide Master**.

10. Send the picture to the **Back**.

11. Change the colour of the **Title Text** to be **light blue**, but **black** on the **Title Master**.

12. Change the fonts on the **Slide Master** and **Title Master**.

13. Apply an **Exciting Animation Scheme** to the all slides.

14. Apply a **Date** to all slides which updates automatically.

15. Add a thick, **light blue** line below the title on all pages of the presentation, except the title page.

16. Set up the slide show to **Loop Continuously**.

17. Print slides 2, 3 and 4 on a single sheet with their associated **Notes** pages.

18. Save the presentation as **Computer Parts** and close it.

Exercise 6.12

1. Open the **Football News** presentation.

2. Add the design template, **Football.pot** from the data files.

3. Change all of the text to **White**.

4. Add a new **Title and Chart** slide to the end of the presentation.

5. Add a title, **Match Performances** to the slide.

6. Edit the chart content to match the following:

	Game 1	Game 2	Game 3	Game 4
Player A	8	6	6	7
Player B	10	9	9	10
Player C	9	10	7	2

7. Change the text associated with the chart to **White**.

6

8. On the **Slide Master** change the **Line Spacing** to **1.5**.

9. Add a **Soccer** image to the top right of every page.

10. Increase the size of the image.

11. Send the image backwards until it appears behind the text.

12. Add **Slow Slide Transitions** to the presentation.

13. Print all of the slides as a handout on a single page.

14. View the slide show.

15. Save the presentation as **Football** and close it.

Exercise 6.13

1. Select **File | New** and use the **AutoContent Wizard** to create a new **Selling a Product or Service** presentation from the **Sales / Marketing** category.

2. Choose to create an on-screen presentation, with the title **New Invention**.

3. Save the presentation as **Invention**.

4. Apply the **Network Design Template**.

5. Display **Outline View**.

6. Move the **Our Strengths** slide above the **Cost Analysis** slide.

7. Delete the **Next Steps** slide.

8. On the **Title Master** insert the **Dots.gif** picture and replace the default image with this one.

9. Add a **Two Colors Gradient** background with different shades of **yellow**.

10. Use the **Set Transparent Color** button, [icon], on the **Pictures** toolbar to remove the **white** from the picture.

11. Change the title font and the colour to **Orange**.

12. Format the **Slide Master** in a similar way, but use a suitable **Preset Gradient Fill Effect**.

13. Insert an **Animated Image** to the top left of the screen by searching for **cogs**.

14. Make this image slightly larger.

15. Reduce the width of the **Title Style** text box to avoid the image.

16. Insert a **Title and Diagram or Organizational Chart** slide after the **Our Strengths** slide.

17. Add an **Organisation Chart** of your choice to this slide and add the title, **Organisation Chart**.

18. Change the orientation of the slides to **Portrait**.

19. Add different slide transitions to each slide.

20. View the presentation.

21. Save the presentation and close it.

Exercise 6.14

1. Open the **Flag Quiz** presentation.

2. Import the image **Ireland Flag.gif** to the space on slide **3**.

3. Insert a text box between the **Greece** and **EU** text and add the text **Ireland**.

4. Change the text colour to **light blue**.

5. Preview slide 3 only.

6. Notice that the new text does not move. Add a **Custom Animation** of a **Custom Line Motion Path** to this text so it moves to the correct position.

7. Preview slide 3 again to check all of the animation.

8. Change the background on the **Slide Master** to a **light blue**.

9. Move back to **Normal** view to see that the text on the flag slides (3-6) is difficult or impossible to see.

10. Draw a long rectangular box around all of the text at the bottom of these 4 slides.

11. Change the fill colour of the box to a **dark blue** and send the box to the **Back**.

12. Apply **Bold** and **Shadow** to the **Title** on the **Master Slide**.

13. Change the bullet style to a **Picture Bullet** of your choice.

14. Display **Slide Sorter** view and move the **European Flags** slide after the **Easy European Flags** slide.

15. Change the text colour on slides **2** and **7** to **black** to ensure it can be read clearly.

16. Insert a suitable picture of a **Globe** into the top right corner of each slide.

17. Move the **Difficult European Flags** to the end of the presentation.

18. Set up the slide show to stop at the 6th slide.

19. Apply **Random Slide Transitions** to the whole presentation.

20. View the whole slide show.

21. Print slide 2 to confirm the rules.

22. Save the presentation as **Flag Quiz Complete** and close it.

Exercise 6.15

1. Create a new, blank presentation.

2. Add the title, **Sport** to the slide.

3. Insert **Text and Title (Bulleted List)** slides with the following titles: **Cricket**, **Tennis**, **Basketball**, **Badminton**.

4. Add a **Clip Art** image to the top right of each of the slides, searching for the appropriate sport name for that slide.

5. Insert a new slide after **Basketball**, titled **Rugby** and add a suitable **Clip Art** image.

6. Add a **Two Color** (2 **greens**) **Diagonal Gradient Fill Effect** to all of the slides.

7. Change all of the fonts on the **Slide Master** to **Impact** and increase the size slightly.

8. Change the colour of the title to a **dark blue** and the other text to **yellow**.

6

9.   Add your name to the **Footer** and the slide number.

10. Add a **Smiley Face AutoShape** to the bottom left of the **Master Slide**.

11. Change the **Fill Colour** of this shape to the **Moss Gradient Effect**.

12. Copy this shape.

13. On the first slide, **Paste** the shape, as many times as required to fill the bottom of the slide.

14. Alter the **Fill Effects** of these shapes to different **Preset Gradients**.

15. Add **Random Slide Transitions** to the presentation.

16. View the slide show.

17. Save the presentation as **Sport**.

18. Close the presentation.

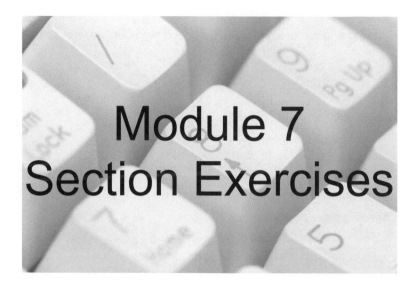

Module 7 Section Exercises

The following revision exercises are divided into sections, each targeted at specific elements of the ECDL/ICDL Syllabus 4 Module 7 Information and Communication. The individual sections are an exact match for the sections in the ECDL/ICDL Syllabus 4 Training Guides from CiA Training, making the guides an ideal reference source for anyone working through these exercises.

7

Revision Exercises

Getting Started

These exercises include topics taken from the following list: understanding the Internet, Being aware of security issues, using *Internet Explorer*, connecting to the Internet, using online help, displaying and removing images and becoming familiar with screens and views.

Exercise 7.1

1.   What makes each website unique?

2.   What type of application is needed to view the Internet?

3.   What program can be used to protect your computer from unauthorized access by others?

4.   Use *IE* help to find out about **connections**.

5.   Where on screen is the address of the webpage you are viewing shown?

6.   Which menu option allows the toolbars in *Internet Explorer* to be changed?

7.   Disconnect from the Internet.

Exercise 7.2

1.   Which 3 buttons in *Internet Explorer* change the page currently being viewed?

2.   What is the **Address Bar** used for in *Internet Explorer*?

3.   Which information will you need from an **ISP** to allow connection to the Internet?

4.   What are viruses?

5.   What is a cache?

6.   View the **Tip of the Day**.

7.   Close *Internet Explorer* and disconnect from the Internet.

Navigation

These exercises include topics taken from the following list: Using hyperlinks, moving backwards and forwards through a website, using web addresses, storing and organising bookmarks, using the history facility and stopping and refreshing downloads.

Exercise 7.3

1.   Go to **www.amazon.co.uk**

2.   Use some of the hyperlinks to browse the different sections of the website.

3.   Go to the books section and create a bookmark.

4.   Now go to **www.wikipedia.org**

5.   Browse using the hyperlinks on the site.

6.   Display the **History** bar.

7.   Look at the entries for the sites you have visited today.

8.   Delete the bookmark you created in step 3.

9.   Clear the browsing history and temporary internet files.

7

Exercise 7.4

1.   Go to **www.weather.co.uk**

2.   Find out the weather for your location.

3.   Go to your default home page.

4.   Use the **Back** button to return to the weather site.

5.   Set a bookmark for this page.

6.   Create a folder called **Weather** and move the bookmark you just created into that folder.

7.   Go to **www.imdb.com** and use the hyperlinks to look around the site.

8.   Delete the **Weather** folder.

Browsing the Web

These exercises include topics taken from the following list: browsing the web using search engines, using subject directories, using the search bar and finding text on a page.

Exercise 7.5

1.   Go to **www.A9.com**

2.   Search for information on the **moon**.

3.   Now alter your search to only display results that contain both the terms **moon** and **landing**.

4. Now go to **www.yahoo.com**

5. Go to the **News** category and browse the headlines.

6. Use the **Back** button to return to the main Yahoo page.

7. Search for **cars** in the **Video** search category.

Exercise 7.6

1. Visit **www.google.com**

2. Search for **Shopping**.

3. Click on the **News** link to view news stories on shopping.

4. Open the **Search bar** and look for information on **ECDL**.

5. Click on one of the hyperlinks displayed.

6. Go to **www.bbc.co.uk** and look for all occurrences of the word **news** on the page.

7. Find a link to world news.

8. Use it to browse some international news items.

Saving and Printing

These exercises include topics taken from the following list: saving a web page, duplicating web page items, modifying page setup, previewing and printing pictures, printing a search result and downloading files.

Exercise 7.7

1. Go to **www.mapquest.com**

2. Go to the **Outside US & Canada** section, if required. Enter your zip/postal code and get the map for where you live.

3. Right click on the map.

4. Save the map to a location on your computer with the name **My House**.

5. Clink on the **Print** link on the page. Preview the page that loads.

6. Change the page setup to landscape and then print it.

Exercise 7.8

1. Go to **www.google.com**

2. Search for **bananas**. Print the first two pages of results.

3. Select one of the results returned to view the page.

4. Save the page as **Banana Page**.

5. Go to **www.downloads.com**.

6. Click on the **Utilities** section.

Note: If you are not working on your <u>own</u> personal computer, make sure you get permission from the owner or your tutor before completing the following steps.

7.   Select one of the links and then download the file from the page that appears, saving it.

8.   View the page saved in step 4.

9.   Delete the saved web page and saved file.

Outlook

These exercises include topics taken from the following list: understanding electronic messaging and related issues, using online help, using e-mail, changing screen display and closing *Outlook*.

Exercise 7.9

1.   Which of the following are valid e-mail addresses?

   a) Jim.Smith@mycompany.com

   b) dave jones@smalltown.co.uk

   c) Jack_Jennings@smalltown.co.uk

   d) billgates@microsoft

2.   Use *Outlook* help to find information on the **address book**.

3.   Add the **Size** field to the headers in the **Inbox**.

4.   Create a folder in the **Inbox** called **Archive**.

5.   Remove the **Size** field from the **Inbox** headers.

7

Exercise 7.10

1.   Open *Outlook*

2.   Display the **Folder List**.

3.   Hide the reading/preview pane.

4.   View the **Inbox**.

5.   Show the reading/preview pane and hide the **Folder List**.

6.   Close *Outlook*

7.   Where is contact information stored in *Outlook*?

8.   What is junk mail?

Message Editing

These exercises include topics taken from the following list: creating a message, inserting and deleting text, using the spell checker, adding a signature to a message, cutting, copying and pasting messages, cutting and pasting from *Word*.

Exercise 7.11

1.   Open *Outlook*.

2.   Create a new signature, including your full name.

3.   Create a new message and write a short paragraph discussing your hobbies.

4.   Select all of the message text and cut it.

5.   Type the following text: **This is a short email about me:**

6.   Leave a few lines after this new line of text and paste your original text back into the message.

7.   Spell check the message. It is now ready to send.

8.   Close *Outlook*.

Exercise 7.12

1.   Open *Word*.

2.   Type this message, including the spelling mistakes:

> **This is my frist email. I shall hopfully be sending you more in the future.**

3.   Insert any suitable clip art picture. Cut the text and the picture.

4.   Open *Outlook* and create a new message.

5.   Paste the text and picture into the new message.

6.   Use the spell checker to correct the spelling mistakes.

7.   Close the message <u>without</u> saving.

8.   Close *Word* <u>without</u> saving.

7

Send and Receive

These exercises include topics taken from the following list: sending, opening and reading messages, attaching files, changing message priority, replying and forwarding messages, using the address book and creating a distribution list.

Exercise 7.13

1. Open *Outlook*.

2. Create a new message. Address it to yourself.

3. Create a *Word* document containing only your name and address.

4. Save it as **File** and close *Word*.

5. Attach this file to your e-mail message.

6. Change the message priority to **High**.

7. Enter the following message:

    This is an email with an attachment.

8. Send the message.

9. Wait a few minutes then check for the new e-mail.

10. Save the attachment, overwriting the original file if prompted.

Exercise 7.14

1. Create a new email addressed to yourself.

2. Enter a subject and message.

3.   Send the message.

4.   When you receive it, forward the message to a friend, adding the text **This is a test to ensure forwarding e-mails works.**

5.   Create four contacts in your address book.

6.   Create a distribution list called **Friends** and add three of the contacts to the list.

7.   Create a new message and address it to the **Friends** list.

8.   Add a subject and a message.

9.   Send the message.

Message Management

These exercises include topics taken from the following list: printing messages, deleting messages and organising messages in folders.

Exercise 7.15

1.   Organise the messages in your **Inbox** by **Importance**.

2.   Print a copy of the first two emails.

3.   Delete any emails received from yourself.

4.   Check to ensure they have moved to the **Deleted Items** folder.

5.   Empty the **Deleted Items** folder.

7

Exercise 7.16

1. Send yourself two e-mails, one with the subject **Important Message**.

2. When the e-mails have been received, search the subject headers for the term **Message**.

3. Create an e-mail folder called **Urgent**.

4. Move the messages found in the search to the **Urgent** folder.

5. Print a message from the **Urgent** folder.

6. Move any e-mails you wish to keep from the **Urgent** folder back to the **Inbox**.

7. Delete the **Urgent** folder.

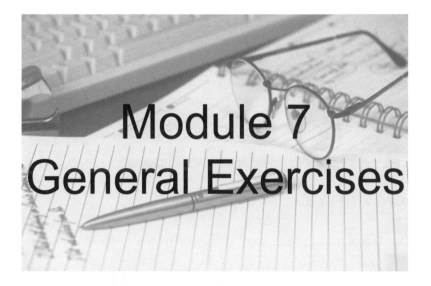

Module 7
General Exercises

The following revision exercises can involve processes from any part of the ECDL/ICDL Syllabus 4 Module 7: Information and Communication.

Exercise 7.17

1. Open your web browser and go to a search engine.

2. Search for the term **ocean** but <u>not</u> for any entries about the **Pacific**. View a few of the results.

3. Create a bookmark for one of the sites.

4. Use your **History** entries to return to one of the pages you previously looked at.

5. Go to the page you bookmarked and save it as **Oceans**.

6. Close your web browser.

7. View the **Oceans** page you saved earlier and print it.

8. What does a padlock in the **Status Bar** of your web browser indicate?

9. Why do you have to be careful when dealing with e-mail attachments?

10. Use *Outlook* help to find information on **message priorities**.

11. Send two e-mails to yourself with different subjects and messages.

12. Wait a few minutes then check for any new e-mails.

13. Read both the e-mails.

14. Flag one of the messages.

15. Mark the other message as being unread.

16. Reply to the e-mail you flagged.

17. Change the priority of the reply to **High**.

18. Write some text in response to the message and send it.

19. When you receive the response delete the original message.

20. Print a copy of the response.

21. Forward the response to yourself including a hyperlink to **www.ciatraining.co.uk** in the message.

22. When this message is received, use the hyperlink to start your web browser and view the page that is displayed.

23. Set this page as your home page.

24. Close *Outlook*.

25. Change your home page as desired.

26. Close your web browser.

Exercise 7.18

1. Go to a search engine in your web browser.

2. Search for images of **boats**.

3. Copy one of the pictures found into a *Word* document and save it, calling it **My Boat**.

4. Go to your home page.

5. Use the **Search Bar** to look for **News**. View one of the sites that are returned.

6. Use the hyperlinks on the site to view some of the current top stories.

7. Use the **Back** button to return to the search engine.

8. Find information on **flights** to **New York**.

9. Print preview the page.

10. Clear your web browser's **History**.

11. Display the folders list in *Outlook*.

12. Create a new message.

13. Give it a subject and message but do not send it.

14. Save the message and close it.

15. View the **Drafts** folder to see this e-mail.

16. Create a new folder called **to be sent**.

17. Move the e-mail from the **Drafts** folder to this new folder.

18. Open the message again.

19. Open the **My Boat** document created earlier. Copy and paste the picture into the message body of the e-mail.

20. Close *Word*.

21. Insert the **My Boat** document as an attachment.

22. Delete the picture from within the message.

Revision Series
© CiA Training Ltd 2005

23. Add message text to instruct the recipient to view the attachment.

24. Send the message to yourself.

25. Delete the **to be sent** folder and the message when you receive it.

26. What indicates an e-mail contains an attachment?

27. What is a domain name?

28. What is a distribution list?

Exercise 7.19

1. What is the Internet?

2. What is the world-wide web?

3. Use your browser to find matches for **online support**.

4. Display your list of favourite sites.

5. Select one of your favourites to view the page.

6. Move one of your favourites to the **Links bar**.

7. Go to a different website. Before the page has fully loaded stop the page loading, then refresh it.

8. Go to **www.ciasupport.co.uk**.

9. Use the links to go to the **Image Gallery** and pick a category from the left of the screen.

7

10. Download an image file from that category. Save it.

11. Delete the temporary internet files and clear the history.

12. What separates the username from the domain name in an e-mail address?

13. Do you have to open an e-mail to read it?

14. If you are using *Outlook Express*, move to step 19.

15. Add the **Due By** field to the headers in the **Inbox**.

16. Set a flag for one of the messages in your **Inbox** and set a due by date and time. The date will now be displayed in the newly added column.

17. Clear the flag.

18. Remove the **Due By** column.

19. Write a message using a text editor. Copy and paste the text into a new message.

20. Spell check the text.

21. Create a signature.

22. Add the signature to the new message.

23. Close *Outlook*.

Revision Series
© CiA Training Ltd 2005

Exercise 7.20

1. In *Internet Explorer* remove the **Address Bar**.

2. Switch to full screen mode.

3. Use your favourites to open another page.

4. Return to normal view.

5. Restore the **Address Bar**.

6. Go to **www.yahoo.com**.

7. Search in one of the categories, e.g. **shopping**, **movies** or **travel**, using the keyword **news** to find news on the chosen category.

8. Find all occurrences of the word **news** on the page.

9. Print preview the results.

10. Print the first and third page of results.

11. What are the advantages of e-mail over the postal system?

12. Change the headers in the **Inbox** to display the **Size** column after the **From** column.

13. Send an e-mail to yourself with a suitable subject and message.

14. When you receive the message, reply to it <u>without</u> including the original message.

15. When the reply is received, add the sender to your address book using your own name as the contact name.

7

16. Set messages being marked as read when displayed in the preview pane after a wait time of 20 seconds.

17. Ensure a message in your **Inbox** is marked as unread. View the message in the preview pane and wait 20 seconds for it to be marked read.

18. Change options so the original message is included when sending replies.

19. Move the **Size** column back to its original position (after the **Received** column).

20. Close *Outlook* using the menu.

21. Where are all newly received messages stored by default?

22. Which of the following is a well known search engine?

      a) **www.microsoft.com**

      b) **www.bbc.co.uk**

      c) **www.google.com**

      d) **www.amazon.com**

23. Which of the following would you use to browse the web?

      a) *Outlook*

      b) *Word*

      c) Firewall

      d) *Internet Explorer*

Exercise 7.21

1. In *Internet Explorer* the collection of icons that perform the most common commands is known as what?

2. What is described by the following text?

   Pieces of coloured text, images or buttons which, when clicked on, take the user to a different page.

3. What is another name for a URL?

4. What is the name given to the first page that is displayed when a website is opened?

5. Create a new folder in the favourites menu called **New Sites**.

6. Travel to two different websites and create bookmarks for both.

7. Move the two new bookmarks into the **New Sites** folder.

8. Rename the **New Sites** folder **My favourite pages**.

9. Remove the **Links bar**.

10. Change the number of days pages are kept in the **History** to **7**.

11. Go to **www.google.com**.

12. Search for the phrase **pieces of eight**.

13. Now search for results where the words **pieces of eight** appear together. Notice the different results for the two methods.

14. Without visiting the site set your home page to **www.bbc.co.uk**.

7

15. Go to the home page of a search engine and search for **beaujolais**. Make a note of how many sites are found.

16. Click the advanced search option. This is an example of a web form.

17. Use the same search: **beaujolais**, but this time specify the search must only be for pages in **English**. Note the number of sites found this time.

18. Open a text editor such as *Word* or *Notepad*. Type the following :

    Best regards,

    Bob Harvey

    Widgets r Us Ltd

19. Go to create a new signature. Cut the text you've just typed and paste it as the text for your signature.

20. Create a new message addressed to yourself. Create some message text then apply the signature (if not done automatically) to finish off the letter.

21. Send the message.

22. When you have received the message, reply, attaching a file of your choice. Enter some message text and send it.

23. When the reply is received, flag the message.

24. Delete the signature and any e-mails from yourself.

25. Close *Outlook* and close your browser if it is still open.

This section contains answers to all specific questions posed in the preceding exercises, together with the name of the file or files containing the worked solution for each exercise.

Revision Exercises

Module 1: Basic Concepts of I.T.

Exercise 1.1

Step 1   c

Step 2   b

Step 3   a

Step 4   d

Step 5   c

Exercise 1.2

Step 1   a

Step 2   d

Step 3   a

Step 4   b

Step 5   c

Step 6   d

Step 7   b

Exercise 1.3

Step 1   d

Step 2   a

Step 3   c

Step 4   a

Step 5   d

Step 6   b

Step 7   c

Revision Series
© CiA Training Ltd 2005

Exercise 1.4

Step 1   b

Step 2   a

Step 3   d

Step 4   c

Step 5   b

Step 6   a

Step 7   d

Exercise 1.5

Step 1   c

Step 2   c

Step 3   a

Step 4   c

Step 5   c

Step 6   d

Step 7   b

Exercise 1.6

Step 1   d

Step 2   c

Step 3   d

Step 4   a

Step 5   b

Step 6   d

Step 7   d

Revision Exercises

Exercise 1.7

Step 1   b

Step 2   c

Step 3   d

Step 4   a

Step 5   d

Step 6   a

Exercise 1.8

Step 1   b

Step 2   a

Step 3   d

Step 4   c

Step 5   a

Step 6   c

Exercise 1.9

Step 1   d

Step 2   b

Step 3   d

Step 4   a

Step 5   d

Step 6   b

Step 7   d

Step 8   b

Revision Series
© CiA Training Ltd 2005

Exercise 1.10

Step 1	d
Step 2	a
Step 3	a
Step 4	d
Step 5	b
Step 6	c
Step 7	c

Exercise 1.11

Step 1	c
Step 2	a
Step 3	c
Step 4	a
Step 5	d

Exercise 1.12

Step 1	d
Step 2	c
Step 3	d
Step 4	d
Step 5	a
Step 6	c

Exercise 1.13

Step 1	c

Step 2   c

Step 3   d

Step 4   a

Exercise 1.14

Step 1   d

Step 2   b

Step 3   c

Step 4   c

Exercise 1.15

Step 1   a

Step 2   b

Step 3   d

Step 4   c

Step 5   b

Step 6   d

Step 7   c

Exercise 1.16

Step 1   b

Step 2   c

Step 3   d

Step 4   a

Step 5   b

Step 6   c

Exercise 1.17

Step 1	b		Step 11	a
Step 2	c		Step 12	b
Step 3	d		Step 13	d
Step 4	b		Step 14	a
Step 5	a and b		Step 15	d
Step 6	b		Step 16	b
Step 7	c		Step 17	c
Step 8	c		Step 18	c
Step 9	d		Step 19	c
Step 10	a		Step 20	c

Exercise 1.18

Step 1	d		Step 11	d
Step 2	d		Step 12	c
Step 3	a		Step 13	a
Step 4	b		Step 14	b
Step 5	a		Step 15	a and c
Step 6	a, b and d		Step 16	b
Step 7	c		Step 17	d
Step 8	a		Step 18	c
Step 9	d		Step 19	a and c
Step 10	c		Step 20	b

Revision Exercises

Exercise 1.19

Step 1	d
Step 2	a
Step 3	b
Step 4	b and c
Step 5	d
Step 6	c
Step 7	d
Step 8	b and c
Step 9	a
Step 10	a
Step 11	c
Step 12	a
Step 13	d
Step 14	c
Step 15	d
Step 16	d
Step 17	a
Step 18	a, b and c
Step 19	a and b
Step 20	d

Exercise 1.20

Step 1	d
Step 2	c
Step 3	b
Step 4	c
Step 5	d
Step 6	a
Step 7	a
Step 8	b and c
Step 9	a
Step 10	d
Step 11	a
Step 12	b
Step 13	c
Step 14	d
Step 15	b
Step 16	a, b, c and d
Step 17	a
Step 18	a and b
Step 19	a and b
Step 20	a and b

Exercise 1.21

Step 1	d	Step 11	a
Step 2	a	Step 12	d
Step 3	d	Step 13	b
Step 4	d	Step 14	a
Step 5	b	Step 15	a
Step 6	a	Step 16	c
Step 7	d	Step 17	d
Step 8	b and c	Step 18	a
Step 9	c	Step 19	a, b and c
Step 10	b	Step 20	a and c

Module 2: Using the Computer and Managing Files

These answers were produced assuming the exercises were worked through in order. There may be slight variations if exercises are attempted out of sequence.

Exercise 2.1

Step 1   Click here to begin.

Step 2   The **Taskbar** is at the bottom of the screen.

Exercise 2.3

Step 6   **10** file types.

Step 8   **27kb**

Step 9   **649kb** (don't include the **General Exercises** folder)

Step 10   **1**, **Countries.htm**.

Exercise 2.4

Step 4   **8** files (**10** if **.tif** files are named *Microsoft Office Document Imaging* files)

Step 5   **5** subfolders (**6** including a *Microsoft Office Document Imaging* folder).

Exercise 2.5

Step 3   **6** or **7** tabs, depending on the printer.

Exercise 2.6

Step 2   The **Add Printer Wizard**.

Step 7   **Sharing**

Exercise 2.7

Step 2   Toolbars.

Step 3   **Font**, **Bullet Style**, **Paragraphs** and **Tabs**.

Step 13

WordPad.rtf	1 KB	Rich Text Format	26/08/2005 12:30
Calculator.rtf	4,542 KB	Rich Text Format	26/08/2005 12:33

Exercise 2.8

Step 2   The **Remove** or **Change/Remove** button.

Exercise 2.9

Step 3   *WordPad* if *Word* is not available.

Step 4   1234

Step 5   3kb

Step 6   8kb

Secret.rtf	8 KB	Rich Text Format	19/08/2005 09:21

Step 8   Yes, the zipped files are the same size.

Exercise 2.10

Step 1   184kb.

Step 2   184kb.

Step 3   File Compression Software.

Step 6   82kb.

Exercise 2.11

Step 1   A piece of malicious coding introduced to a computer system, with the ability to spread itself to other computers.

Step 2   No. Viruses can cause many different kinds of damage from annoyance to destruction.

Step 3   Yes. Viruses can be passed via a file from a floppy disk or CD.

Step 4   Installing software from an unreliable source.
Opening a file containing a virus.
E-mail attachments.

Step 5   E-mail attachments.

Step 6   **Scan** and **Shield**.

Exercise 2.12

Step 2   A wide range, from annoyance to real damage, e.g. deleting file.

Step 3   Disinfecting is the process removing all traces of a discovered virus and where possible, reversing their effects.

Step 4   Possible sources of infection are automatically checked for viruses and reported on. Some can check incoming and outgoing e-mail for viruses before it has been processed by the computer.

Step 5   It cannot detect new viruses which are not on the list.

Step 6   Automatically online.

Exercise 2.15

Step 11

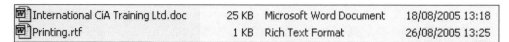

Step16

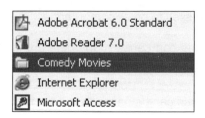

Exercise 2.16

Step 3   **27kb**.

Step 6   Smaller. The zipped file can fit on a floppy disk.

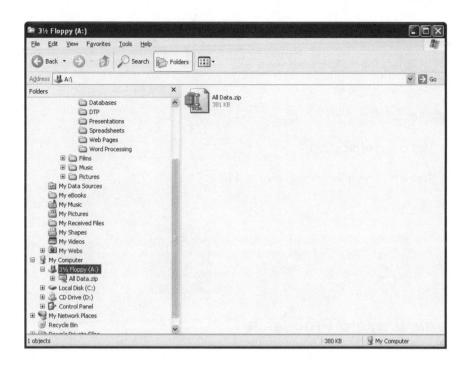

Exercise 2.17

Step 16

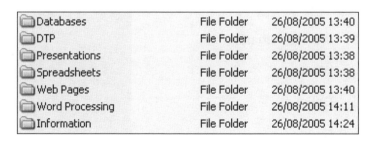

3 Screens.rtf	4,038 KB	Rich Text Format	26/08/2005 14:11

Exercise 2.18

Step 4

Databases	File Folder	26/08/2005 13:40
DTP	File Folder	26/08/2005 13:39
Presentations	File Folder	26/08/2005 13:38
Spreadsheets	File Folder	26/08/2005 13:38
Web Pages	File Folder	26/08/2005 13:40
Word Processing	File Folder	26/08/2005 14:11
Information	File Folder	26/08/2005 14:24

Step 6

CiA Training International Info.doc	25 KB	Microsoft Word Document	18/08/2005 13:18

Exercise 2.19

Step 5   **Tropical.zip**.

Step 8   The difference in size is 116kb.

Step 10

Module 3: Word Processing

Exercise 3.1

Step 6   d, **Image** is not a toolbar.

Step 7   Tooltips.

Step 8   False, toolbars can be displayed anywhere.

Step 9   None, all options are active.

Exercise 3.2

Step 3   **View | Toolbars**.

Step 5   **Windows**.

Step 5   **Options**.

Step 6   No.

Exercise 3.3

Step 3   The message will ask - **Do you want to save the changes to this document**. The exact wording will vary with the application version.

Step 5   **.doc**

Step 6   **.rtf**

Exercise 3.4

Step 5   **.htm**

Step 8   **.txt**

Step 9   Because any formatting in the original document may be lost.

Exercise 3.5

Step 3   b

Step 6   **<Ctrl> + click**.

Step 8   The deleted sentence reappears.

A sample solution for this exercise is saved as **Gardens2 Solution** in the **Module 3 Solutions** folder.

Exercise 3.6

Step 8   The required keys are **<Ctrl> + A**.

Step 9   All text is deleted and replaced with the letter q.

A sample solution for this exercise is saved as **Ballet2 Solution** in the **Module 3 Solutions** folder.

Revision Exercises

Exercise 3.7

Step 8   Zoom is at 100%

Step 9   **Multiple Pages** button.

Exercise 3.8

Step 8   The font size of the text has been reduced.

Exercise 3.9

A sample solution for this exercise is saved as **Lakes2 Solution** in the **Module 3 Solutions** folder.

Exercise 3.10

A sample solution for this exercise is saved as **Banks2 Solution** in the **Module 3 Solutions** folder.

Exercise 3.12

Step 2   Text is too small to read

Step 3   Cannot see much of the page.

Step 5   Toffington, Tarquin and Twiste.

Step 6   4 replacements are made.

Exercise 3.13

A sample solution for this exercise is saved as **Lakes3 Solution** in the **Module 3 Solutions** folder.

Revision Series
© CiA Training Ltd 2005

Exercise 3.14

A sample solution for this exercise is saved as **List2 Solution** in the **Module 3 Solutions** folder.

Exercise 3.15

Step 2   The **Windows** menu.

A sample solution for this exercise is saved as **Gardens3 Solution** in the **Module 3 Solutions** folder.

Exercise 3.16

Step 2   Only in **Print Layout** view.

A sample solution for this exercise is saved as **Rocks2 Solution** in the **Module 3 Solutions** folder.

Exercise 3.17

A sample solution for this exercise is saved as **Mountains Solution** in the **Module 3 Solutions** folder.

Exercise 3.18

A sample solution for this exercise is saved as **Log Solution** in the **Module 3 Solutions** folder.

Exercise 3.19

A sample solution for this exercise is saved as **Lakes4 Solution** in the **Module 3 Solutions** folder.

Exercise 3.20

Step 9   Only 1.

Step 10   Portrait and Landscape.

A sample solution for this exercise is saved as **Hall2 Solution** in the **Module 3 Solutions** folder.

Exercise 3.21

Sample solutions for this exercise are saved as **Offers Solution** and **Letters3 Solution** in the **Module 3 Solutions** folder.

Exercise 3.22

A sample solution for this exercise is saved as **Letters4 Solution** in the **Module 3 Solutions** folder.

Exercise 3.23

Step 10   Any corner handle.

A sample solution for this exercise is saved as **Ballet3 Solution** in the **Module 3 Solutions** folder.

Exercise 3.24

A sample solution for this exercise is saved as **Outdoor Solution** in the **Module 3 Solutions** folder.

Exercise 3.25

Sample solutions for this exercise are saved as **Offers Solution** and **Letters3 Solution** in the **Module 3 Solutions** folder.

Exercise 3.26

A sample solution for this exercise is saved as **Holiday Plan2 Solution** in the **Module 3 Solutions** folder.

Exercise 3.27

Sample solutions for this exercise are saved as **Thanksmerge Solution** and **Report2 Solution** in the **Module 3 Solutions** folder.

Exercise 3.28

Step 8

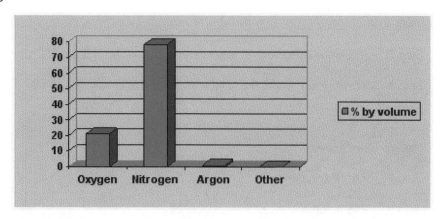

A sample solution for this exercise is saved as **Science2 Solution** in the **Module 3 Solutions** folder.

Exercise 3.29

Sample solutions for this exercise are saved as **Appointment Letters Solution** and **Questionnaire2 Solution** in the **Module 3 Solutions** folder.

Module 4: Spreadsheets

Exercise 4.1

Step 3   a) **Paste** b) **Print Preview** c) **Copy** d) **Format Painter**

Step 4   **7** items.

Step 6   **Add-ins** are programs that add optional commands and features to *Microsoft Excel*.

Step 8   Selected **File | Exit** or clicked the **Close** button.

Exercise 4.2

Step 2   a) **Cut** b) **AutoSum** c) **Insert Hyperlink** d) **Merge and Center**

Step 4   **<End →>** or **<Ctrl →>**. The last column is column **IV**.

Step 5   **65536**

Step 6   **<Home>**

Step 7   **<Alt Page Down>**

Step 9   **255** columns

Step 10   4 different ways: a) **File | Exit** b) window **Close** button (top right) c) key press **<Alt F4>** d) right click on window control icon (top left) and select **Close**.

Exercise 4.3

Step 2   Cell **N31**

Step 3   Range of Booking block **Q3:AF9**

Step 4   **35%**

Step 6   **Payments**

Step 8   **9800**

Exercise 4.4

Step 4   **Market Stall**

Step 7   **Temperatures**

Step 9   Cell **N14**

Step 10   The key press is <**Ctrl Home**>

Exercise 4.6

A sample solution for this exercise is saved as **Adelaide Weather Solution.htm** in the **Module 4 Solutions** folder.

Exercise 4.7

Step 2   **49**

Step 3   **37**

Step 5   **Column of numbers**

Step 6   **143**

Step 7   **143**. **Yes** the answers are the same

A sample solution for this exercise is saved as **Courses Solution** in the **Module 4 Solutions** folder.

Exercise 4.8

Step 6   **2225** profit

Step 7   **John** made the most profit for the company, 545

A sample solution for this exercise is saved as **Computer Sales Solution** in the **Module 4 Solutions** folder.

Exercise 4.9

Step 2   c) more than 1000 under - too pessimistic.
A sample solution for this exercise is saved as **Forecast2 Solution** in the **Module 4 Solutions** folder.

Exercise 4.10

A sample solution for this exercise is saved as **Divisions2 Solution** in the **Module 4 Solutions** folder.

Exercise 4.11

Step 5   14.55

Step 9   1.40 short

A sample solution for this exercise is saved as **Petty Cash Feb Solution** in the **Module 4 Solutions** folder.

Exercise 4.12

Step 3   -25

Step4   Ali

Step 7   Numbers are sorted first

Step 9   4 replacements were made

Step 11   2AC

Step 12   Case has no effect when being sorted

Exercise 4.13

Step 3   &[File]

Exercise 4.14

Step 2   The worksheet is previewed over 6 pages

Exercise 4.15

Step 6   78850

Step 7   New York

Step 8   Saturday

A sample solution for this exercise is saved as **Theatre2 Solution** in the **Module 4 Solutions** folder.

Exercise 4.16

Step 8   The orientation is **Portrait** and it has **2** pages.

A sample solution for this exercise is saved as **Market Stall Formatted Solution** in the **Module 4 Solutions** folder.

Exercise 4.17

Step 8   The Average is **1244.37**.

A sample solution for this exercise is saved as **Stationery Sales Solution** in the **Module 4 Solutions** folder.

Exercise 4.18

Step 4   The average mark is 60.

Step 5   The average now is 64.

Step 13   14 passes.

A sample solution for this exercise is saved as **Results2 Solution** in the **Module 4 Solutions** folder.

Exercise 4.19

Step 4   The row will not adjust automatically because the row was manually adjusted in step 3.

A sample solution for this exercise is saved as **Chart Solution** in the **Module 4 Solutions** folder.

Exercise 4.20

Step 4   **Sydney** with an average temperature of **19.4**.

Step 12   Toronto has a colder winter but a warmer summer compared to London.

A sample solution for this exercise is saved as **Temperature Chart Solution** in the **Module 4 Solutions** folder.

Exercise 4.21

Step 18   The percentage profit is **20.3%**.

A sample solution for this exercise is saved as **Holiday Cottages Solution** in the **Module 4 Solutions** folder.

Exercise 4.22

Step 22   The best selling wine is the **Riesling White** (stock code **W02**).

A sample solution for this exercise is saved as **Wine Warehouse Solution** in the **Module 4 Solutions** folder.

Exercise 4.23

Step 7   There are **26** entries.

Step 12   The prize fund is **1800**.

Step 17   The **First Place** prize money is **39%** of the total.

A sample solution for this exercise is saved as **Tournament Results Solution** in the **Module 4 Solutions** folder.

Exercise 4.24

A sample solution for this exercise is saved as **World Cup2 Solution** in the **Module 4 Solutions** folder.

Exercise 4.25

Step 11   **60cm**. Tanks 5 and 6.

Step 12   **6** tanks are too small.

Step 14   Cost is **65**.

Step 16   **Tank 10**.

Step 17   **Angel** fish - not enough depth, **Clown Barb** not enough volume of water and probably the **Discus** fish as it needs a large tank.

Step 31   The tank is **47%** of the cost.

A sample solution for this exercise is saved as **Tropical Fish Solution** in the **Module 4 Solutions** folder.

Module 5: Databases

Exercise 5.1

Step 3   There are **2** tables, **Computers** and **Repairs**.

Step 4   Ghosted options are **Save** and **Page Setup**.

Step 5   **AutoNumber** primary keys, **Single-field** primary keys, and **Multiple-field** primary keys.

Step 6   **Relationships**.

Step 7   There is **1** macro.

Step 8   **c**, both *Access* and the database will close.

Exercise 5.2

Step 4   **40** records, this value is shown next to the navigation buttons.

Step 5   **14** fields for each record.

Step 6   12 Desert Road.

Step 7   **Subdatasheet** is ghosted.

Step 8   **c** and **d**, adding a new field and changing the column width.

Exercise 5.3

Step 3   Data type changed to **Text** and field size changed to **6**.

Step 4   The primary key must provide a unique reference to the record.

Step 10   **CH004** is the first record because the table is automatically indexed on the primary key field (course ID).

A sample solution for this exercise is saved as **Learning Solution** in the **Module 5 Solutions** folder.

Exercise 5.4

Step 3   The generated primary key is an **AutoNumber** field called **ID**.

Step 9   Records are displayed in **Room No** order because they are indexed on this field.

A sample solution for this exercise is saved as **Hotel Solution** in the **Module 5 Solutions** folder.

Exercise 5.5

Step 6   There are 3 bookings for apartment **B8**.

Step 8   **You cannot add or change a record because a related record is required in table 'Apartments'**, i.e. there is no **B9** record in the apartments table. This is caused by the referential integrity setting.

A sample solution for this exercise is saved as **Sunshine Solution** in the **Module 5 Solutions** folder.

Exercise 5.6

Step 4   Option **b** is false, all others are true.

Step 6   Jason Myers has 14 claims but only for **2** different projects.

Step 8   The relationship is one-to-one because **Staff No** is the primary key in each table and therefore must be unique in each table.

A sample solution for this exercise is saved as **Consultants Solution** in the **Module 5 Solutions** folder.

Exercise 5.7

Step 5   Match setting is **Any Part of Field**. **2** records are found.

Step 6   Key press is **<Ctrl '>** (control and apostrophe together).

A sample solution for this exercise is saved as **Beauty Solution** in the **Module 5 Solutions** folder.

Exercise 5.8

A sample solution for this exercise is saved as **Club Solution** in the **Module 5 Solutions** folder.

Exercise 5.9

Step 3   **27.50**.

Step 4   **27/07/2004**.

Step 6   **130** records are for expenses other than mileage.

Step 7   **11** records are for expenses greater than 1000.

Step 8   Employee **112** has submitted a claim for entertaining against Global.

Exercise 5.10

Step 3   There are **32** premises not in the Central Area.

Step 5   6 Shore Road is the least expensive property in the Riverside Complex.

Step 6   **17** properties are Office Premises and of them, **M017** has the largest area.

Step 8   The previous filter is reapplied, the previous sort is not.

Step 9   **8** unoccupied properties are priced at more than 100,000.

Exercise 5.11

A sample solution for this exercise is included in the **Expenses Solution** in the **Module 5 Solutions** folder.

Exercise 5.12

A sample solution for this exercise is included in the **Central Solution** in the **Module 5 Solutions** folder.

Exercise 5.13

Step 5   The Wizard, **Members2**, assigns different sizes to the data fields on the form. In Design View, **Members3**, all data fields have the same default size.

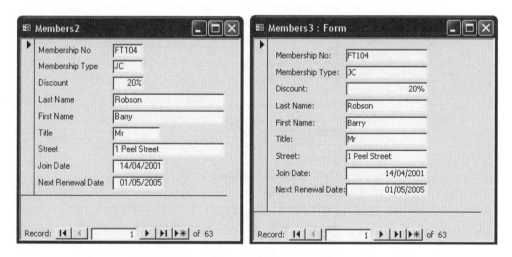

A sample solution for this exercise is included in **Club Solution** in the **Module 5 Solutions** folder.

Exercise 5.14

Step 9   There should be five records on a page, depending on the size of the form.

Properties Form

Premises ID	M001	Disabled Access	Yes
Location	Valley Grove	Comment	Recent Acquisition
Address	Unit 27		
Occupied	No	Floors	1
Type of Premises	Stand Unit	Lift	No
Price	£50,000.00	Parking Spaces	35
Unit Area	78		

Premises ID	M002	Disabled Access	No
Location	Central Area	Comment	Fully Furnished
Address	10 Willow Road		
Occupied	Yes	Floors	3
Type of Premises	Office Premises	Lift	Yes
Price	£75,000.00	Parking Spaces	3
Unit Area	60		

Premises ID	M003	Disabled Access	No
Location	Valley Grove	Comment	Quick Sale
Address	Unit 68		
Occupied	Yes	Floors	1
Type of Premises	Stand Unit	Lift	No
Price	£45,000.00	Parking Spaces	3
Unit Area	150		

Premises ID	M004	Disabled Access	Yes
Location	Enterprise Centre	Comment	Premier Location
Address	88 Kingsway		
Occupied	No	Floors	2
Type of Premises	Office Premises	Lift	Yes
Price	£175,000.00	Parking Spaces	25
Unit Area	167		

Premises ID	M005	Disabled Access	No
Location	Industrial Park	Comment	A good relocation buy
Address	Unit 12 Bridge Court		
Occupied	No	Floors	1
Type of Premises	Manufacturing Unit	Lift	No
Price	£97,000.00	Parking Spaces	6
Unit Area	55		

This diagram is to show layout only. Don't worry if you can't read the details.

A sample solution for this exercise is included in **Central Solution** in the **Module 5 Solutions** folder.

Exercise 5.15

Step 4   **Date** and **Page Number** are shown by default in the page footer.

Department Listing

Department	Surname	Staff No	First Name	Cost
Analyst	Lee	301	Clara	£55.00
Analyst	Morris	403	Tracy	£65.00
Analyst	Oman	205	Tariq	£60.00
Analyst	Shanter	355	David	£50.00
Analyst	Singh	536	Vikram	£55.00
Analyst	Tremble	356	Sue	£50.00
Support	Ametsi	422	Shola	£67.50
Support	Bakewell	214	Jean	£50.00
Support	Crown	108	Thomas	£80.00
Support	Ferguson	244	Terry	£70.00
Support	Kline	505	William	£80.00
Support	Myers	112	Jason	£67.70
Support	Odara	201	Marie	£62.50
Support	Ripley	688	Ellen	£57.50
Support	Svenson	348	Lars	£57.50
Training	Chapman	321	Ian	£55.00
Training	Lister	456	Arnold	£60.00
Training	Longman	126	John	£55.00

19 August 2005   *Page 1 of 2*

A sample solution for this exercise is included in **Expenses Solution** in the **Module 5 Solutions** folder.

Exercise 5.16

Step 7   Property **PO15** is the cheapest in **DockLand**.

Step 9   Grand totals are for all records regardless of how they are grouped so should be the same.

Revision Exercises

```
19 August 2005

Location              Price  Premises ID  Address                      Type of Premises    Occupied
Central Area
                  £56,000.00  P010         The Lothian Suites           Conference Unit     No
                  £75,000.00  M002         10 Willow Road               Office Premises     Yes
                 £100,000.00  M006         16 Station Road              Office Premises     Yes
                 £100,000.00  M014         12th Floor, Stanton Tower     Office Premises     No
                 £156,000.00  P012         17 Hartson Chambers          Office Premises     No
                 £200,000.00  P001         15 Lothian Enterprise Building Office Premises    No
                 £250,000.00  M011         5th Floor, Stanton Tower      Office Premises     No
                 £300,000.00  M012         Raby Exhibition Hall          Exhibition Hall     Yes
Summary for 'Location' = Central Area (8 detail records)
Sum              1237000
DockLand
                  £38,000.00  P015         17 The Port Buildings        Store Unit          Yes
                  £75,000.00  P003         14a The Union Buildings      Manufacturing Unit  No
                  £80,000.00  P004         Unit 7 Grantham House        Manufacturing Unit  Yes
                  £92,000.00  P019         4 Grainger Dock              Manufacturing Unit  No
                 £120,000.00  M010         1 Wessington Road            Manufacturing Unit  Yes
                 £120,000.00  P017         Suite 15 Grosvenor Estate    Store Unit          No
Summary for 'Location' = DockLand (6 detail records)
Sum              525000
Enterprise Centre

Location Analysis                                                                    Page 1 of 3
```

The diagram above is to show layout. Don't worry if you can't read it. A sample solution for this exercise is included in **Central Solution** in the **Module 5 Solutions** folder.

Exercise 5.17

Step 12

	Atomic Number	Name	Symbol	Melting Point
▶	11	Sodium	Na	98
	15	Phosphorus	P	44
	19	Potassium	K	64
	31	Gallium	Ga	30
*	0			0

Melt : Select Query

Step 16 **One to one** link is created. Atomic number is a primary key (and therefore unique) in both tables.

A sample solution for this exercise is saved as **Chemistry Solution** in the **Module 5 Solutions** folder.

Exercise 5.18

Booking List

Start Date by Month	Vehicle Number	Start Date	Number of Days	Type	Charge	Cost
June 2006						
	212	29/06/2006	4	Family	£75	£300.00
	211	29/06/2006	3	Compact	£50	£150.00
Summary for 'Start Date' = 29/06/2006 (2 detail records)						
Sum			7			
July 2006						
	214	02/07/2006	5	Sports	£90	£450.00
	313	03/07/2006	7	Compact	£50	£350.00
Summary for 'Start Date' = 03/07/2006 (2 detail records)						
Sum			12			
Grand Total			19			

19 August 2005   Bill Barnacle

The diagram above is to show layout. Don't worry if you can't read it. A sample solution for this exercise is saved as **Hire Solution** in the **Module 5 Solutions** folder.

Exercise 5.19

Step 2   In **Staff No** sequence because this is the primary key and therefore indexed.

Step 12

Old Testers : Select Query						
Staff No	Department	Surname	First Name	Start Date	Age	Rate
10	Testing	Bluebell	Neil	22/07/1998	57	£17.00

A sample solution for this exercise is saved as **Wages Solution** in the **Module 5 Solutions** folder.

Exercise 5.20

Step 6   Because **Month** is a text field and is therefore sorted alphabetically.

Step 14   **Thraddle** production exceeded **4000** in **March**.

Step 18   **November** has the highest total (12,928) and the overall output for the year is 119,559.

Step 14   **Thraddle** production exceeded **4000** in **March**.

Step 19

Output by Product

Product	Month No	Month	Quantity
Sprange			
	1	January	3784
	2	February	3541
	3	March	3780
	4	April	3137
	5	May	3114
	6	June	2630
	7	July	2585
	8	August	2149
	9	September	3275
	10	October	3690
	11	November	4255
	12	December	4369
Summary for 'Product' = Sprange (12 detail records)			
Sum			40309
Avg			3359.0833

A sample solution for this exercise is saved as **Production Solution** in the **Module 5 Solutions** folder.

Exercise 5.21

Step 3   Mount Kenya was first climbed in 1899.

Step 5   They are all in Asia.

Step 9   6 of the mountains listed are between 5000 and 7000 metres high.

Step 12   6 records can be viewed.

A sample solution for this exercise is saved as **Geography Solution** in the **Module 5 Solutions** folder.

Module 6: Presentations

Exercise 6.1

Step 2   The **Menu Bar**.

Step 4a   **Rectangle** (on the **Drawing** toolbar)

Step 4b   **Bold**

Step 4c   **Paste**

Step 4d   **Rotate Left** (**Picture** toolbar)

Step 5   Select **Slide Show | Slide Transition**, then choose the correct option.

Exercise 6.2

Step 5   Recolours the picture.

Exercise 6.3

A sample solution for this exercise is saved as **Computers2 Solution** in the **Module 6 Solutions** folder.

Exercise 6.4

A sample solution for this exercise is saved as **Planets Solution** in the **Module 6 Solutions** folder.

Exercise 6.5

A sample solution for this exercise is saved as **Computer Formatted Solution** in the **Module 6 Solutions** folder.

Exercise 6.6

A sample solution for this exercise is saved as **Shower Formatted Solution** in the **Module 6 Solutions** folder.

Exercise 6.7

A sample solution for this exercise is saved as **Images Solution** in the **Module 6 Solutions** folder.

Exercise 6.8

A sample solution for this exercise is saved as **Shower2 Solution** in the **Module 6 Solutions** folder.

Exercise 6.9

A sample solution for this exercise is saved as **Computers3 Solution** in the **Module 6 Solutions** folder.

Exercise 6.10

A sample solution for this exercise is saved as **Ocean Fish Solution** in the **Module 6 Solutions** folder.

Exercise 6.11

A sample solution for this exercise is saved as **Computer Parts Solution** in the **Module 6 Solutions** folder.

Exercise 6.12

A sample solution for this exercise is saved as **Football Solution** in the **Module 6 Solutions** folder.

Exercise 6.13

A sample solution for this exercise is saved as **Invention Solution** in the **Module 6 Solutions** folder.

Exercise 6.14

A sample solution for this exercise is saved as **Flag Quiz Complete Solution** in the **Module 6 Solutions** folder.

Exercise 6.15

A sample solution for this exercise is saved as **Sport Solution** in the **Module 6 Solutions** folder.

Module 7: Information & Communication

Exercise 7.1

Step 1   Each has its own unique address.

Step 2   A web browser.

Revision Exercises

Step 3   A firewall.

Step 5   **Address Bar**.

Step 6   **View | Toolbars**.

Exercise 7.2

Step 1   **Home**, **Back**, and **Forward**.

Step 2   To type in website addresses of websites you wish to visit and view the address of the current website.

Step 3   A username and password.

Step 4   Programs which can be downloaded from the Internet, or from other sources that are intended to harm your computer.

Step 5   It is where temporary internet files are stored on your computer.

Exercise 7.9

Step 1   a, c

Exercise 7.10

Step 7   The address book.

Step 8   Unwanted/unsolicited e-mail.

Exercise 7.17

Step 8   The connection is secure/encrypted.

Step 9   E-mail attachments can contain viruses.

Exercise 7.18

Step 26   There is a symbol of a paper clip in the attachment column.

Step 27   The address of the computer that sends and receives mail.

Step 28   A list of specific contacts that will all receive any email sent to the list name.

Exercise 7.19

Step 1   A vast network of computers.

Step 2   The network of information contained on the Internet.

Step 12   The '@' symbol.

Step 13   You can also view it in the preview pane/reading pane.

Exercise 7.20

Step 11   It is faster to be delivered, documents can be transmitted rather than by a courier so it is cheaper. Also it can be accessed from anywhere.

Step 21   In the **Inbox**.

Step 22   c)

Step 23   d)

Exercise 7.21

Step 1   The toolbar.

Step 2   Hyperlinks.

Step 3   A web address.

Step 4   The home page.

Other Products from CiA Training

If you have enjoyed using this guide you can obtain other products from our range of over 150 titles. CiA Training Ltd is a leader in developing self-teach training materials and courseware.

Open Learning Guides

Teach yourself by working through them in your own time. Our range includes products for: Windows, Word, Excel, Access, PowerPoint, Project, Publisher, Internet Explorer, FrontPage and many more… We also have a large back catalogue of products; please call for details.

ECDL/ICDL

We produce accredited training materials for the European Computer Driving Licence (ECDL/ICDL) and the Advanced ECDL/ICDL qualifications. The standard level consists of seven modules and the advanced level four modules. Material produced covers a variety of Microsoft Office products from Office 97 to 2003.

ECDL/ICDL Advanced Revision Series

Consists of a series of four books: AM3 Word Processing, AM4 Spreadsheets, AM5 Database, AM6 Presentation. The revision booklets include topic specific exercises and general exercises covering the whole syllabus for each module.

e-Citizen

Courseware for this exciting new qualification is available now. Students will become proficient Internet users and participate confidently in all major aspects of the online world with the expert guidance of this handbook. Simulated web sites are also supplied for safe practice before tackling the real thing.

Trainer's Packs

Specifically written for use with tutor led I.T. courses. The trainer is supplied with a trainer guide (step by step exercises), course notes (for delegates), consolidation exercises (for use as reinforcement) and course documents (course contents, pre-course questionnaires, evaluation forms, certificate template, etc). All supplied on CD with rights to edit and copy the documents.

Online Shop

To purchase or browse the CiA catalogue please visit, *www.ciatraining.co.uk*.